Praise for *The Whisper Way*

"*The Whisper Way* is a practical, tactical guide for building a business, combined with delightful storytelling."

—Sheryl Sandberg, founder of Lean In

"Carrie truly is the Exit Whisperer—and this book is your secret to cashing in on the business you've poured your heart and soul into."

—Rebecca Minkoff, designer, cofounder of the Female Founder Collective, and author of *Fearless: The New Rules for Creativity, Courage, and Success*

"Carrie has a bold, brave formula for women looking to sell their businesses, and *The Whisper Way* is an actionable guide to making it all happen."

—Reshma Saujani, founder of Girls Who Code and Moms First

"If you want to build a business that is sellable, there is only one book you need to read, and it's the one you're reading right now."

—Kass Lazerow, entrepreneur, investor, venture capitalist, nd author

"Exiting the traditional way isn't always the best way. Discover fresh, unconventional approaches you won't find in a textbook—but you will right here in Carrie's book."

—Shelley Zalis, founder and CEO of The Female Quotient

"Growing, scaling, and selling a company is messy. I wish this book was around when I was exiting my company. It is literally a guidebook for women looking to scale and sell. Can't recommend it enough."

—Alli Webb, author and cofounder of Drybar

"Carrie Kerpen has written the ultimate guide for women on how to scale and sell their businesses with the best strategy there is—sisterhood. Honest, authentic, fun, and filled with brilliant, must-have advice, this book will be every female founder's beach read, guaranteed."

—Jessica Zweig, serial entrepreneur and national bestselling author of *Be*

"*The Whisper Way* is GENIUS. Carrie Kerpen has written the ultimate business book for women entrepreneurs that is distinctively relatable, empathetic, practical, and grounded—and is all of that in a fictionalized narrative format that makes *The Whisper Way* uniquely easy and enjoyable to read. Ramona's retreat will become every woman's fantasy! I've said for years I want women to unashamedly set out to make an absolute goddamn fucking shit-ton of money—Carrie has given all of us the simple-to-follow road map to close the exit gap and do just that. I cannot recommend this book too highly. Buy it now, buy it for all your friends, buy it for your daughters. *The Whisper Way* is the women's wealth generator of the future."

—Cindy Gallop, founder of Make Love Not Porn

"*The Whisper Way* is the blueprint creators have been waiting for—showing exactly how to transform a successful brand into a life-changing exit. Carrie Kerpen doesn't just talk theory; she provides a practical road map for turning influence into generational wealth. This isn't just another business book—it's essential reading for any creator ready to transform their impact into lasting legacy."

—Brittany Hennessy, entrepreneur and author of *Influencer*

"*The Whisper Way* is a story of women who come together to workshop their way toward acquisition. It's told in a fun, interesting way, and highlights the collective power of what happens when brilliant women come together."

—Lindsay Kaplan, cofounder of Chief

"Carrie's energy and enthusiasm for helping female founders is infectious and her experience is unparalleled. Selling your business is the most epic finish line ever and this book is a total game changer."

—Randi Zuckerberg, entrepreneur, author, and ultramarathon runner

"This book is a blueprint for how to scale and sell your business, told from the mindset of a female entrepreneur, which is so inspiring."

—James Dumoulin, founder of the School of Hard Knocks

"Entrepreneurial queens take note: *The Whisper Way* shatters the silence around your potential, revealing a strategic playbook to seize control, transform your business into a million-dollar asset, and catapult your brand legacy. Part parable, part revolution—this is how you claim your throne."

—Aliza Licht, founder of Leave Your Mark and author of *On Brand*

"Carrie sheds the stigma of the term lifestyle business—and teaches you that the business you built to live your life can become a life-changing asset!"

—Stephanie Cartin, author, entrepreneur, and cofounder of Entreprenista

THE
WHISPER
WAY

Also by Carrie Kerpen

Work It: Secrets for Success from the Boldest Women in Business

THE WHISPER WAY

The Secret Formula *for*
Women Entrepreneurs *to* Scale *and* Sell
for Life-Changing Money

CARRIE KERPEN

BenBella Books, Inc.
Dallas, TX

The Whisper Way copyright © 2025 by Caroline Kerpen

BenBella Books, Inc.
8080 N. Central Expressway, Suite 1700
Dallas, TX 75206
www.benbellabooks.com
Send feedback to feedback@benbellabooks.com

BenBella is a federally registered trademark.

Printed in the United States of America
10 9 8 7 6 5 4 3 2 1

Library of Congress Control Number: 2024052022
ISBN 9781637746745 (hardcover)
ISBN 9781637746752 (electronic)

Editing by Claire Schulz
Copyediting by Natalie Roth
Proofreading by Rebecca Maines and Lisa Story
Text design and composition by PerfecType, Nashville, TN
Vision board image created by Noah Cohen
Cover design by Brigid Pearson
Printed by Lake Book Manufacturing

This book is dedicated to my mother, Judy Fisher.
You would have been an amazing entrepreneur, Mom.
And to Charlotte, Kate, Seth, and Dave.
You are my everything.

Contents

Introduction

Dear Female Founders,

In 2007, I started an agency business with $10,000 in the bank and zero experience as an entrepreneur. Fourteen years later, I sold that business for eight figures. I sold to a great company, at a healthy multiple. Some might say it was a fairy-tale exit.

My typical MO would be to downplay this accomplishment. You'll find a lot of interviews where I say it was an accident, it was a lot of luck and good timing. I also say I had a lot of help from my incredible network. I talk a lot about my husband/cofounder, who was, and still is, a visionary, and how I couldn't have done it without him.

All of that is absolutely true.

And.

I have been well trained on answers that convey relatability and likeability. After all, the company I built and sold was literally called "Likeable." My entire brand is about being authentic, approachable, and the nice gal who can do it all.

And something else is also true about my journey. I may have started as an anxious, "accidental" entrepreneur because I wanted to have the freedom of time that being your own boss allows. But over time, I became a calculated, strategic, financially savvy leader.

Actually, I might have been that leader all along.

Still, as much as I know that about myself, it still feels uncomfortable to say. Even as I write it, I think, *Were you really, though?*

Yes. Yes, I was.

This book is a love letter to every woman entrepreneur I know. Every woman entrepreneur who has ever doubted herself. Every woman who questions if she can go big. Every woman who intentionally wants to keep her business small and manageable. Every woman who started a company to own her own time, but who now feels owned by that company. Every woman who eventually wants to sell her business but has no idea where to start. Every female founder struggling to articulate exactly what she wants. And every woman who knows *exactly* what she wants from her business but has no idea how to get there. This book is for you.

I got the idea for this book after I sold Likeable. The sale process was scary, and arduous. If you ever experience imposter syndrome, there's no deeper way to reinforce that feeling than to have someone go line by line through your financials and your business plans, questioning their veracity. I sat in due diligence meetings, surrounded entirely by men (with the exception of my incredible female advisor—thanks, Amanda!), defending the value of my business. While I was doing that, I was also dealing with the emotional impact of selling something that was an actual part of me. It felt like I was fighting to sell my left arm, or even my child.

I learned so much through that process, but two core lessons stand out:

- One, I built an incredibly healthy, sellable business.
- Two, women business owners have different experiences when it comes to growing, valuing, and exiting their businesses than men.

Oh boy, do people react when I mention that second one. Men hate it, and some women hate it, too. We want to believe that we have the exact same opportunities as men and that there are no differences in what we are capable of. And while we certainly are capable, the journey is unquestionably more difficult. This doesn't just apply to entrepreneurship. It's different in most aspects of life. Cartoonist Bob Thaves summarized this perfectly in his *Frank and Ernest* cartoon series. In one cartoon, Frank and Ernest are staring at a billboard announcing a Fred Astaire film festival. The caption reads: "Sure he was great, but don't forget that Ginger Rogers did everything he did . . . backwards and in high heels."

We can do anything men can do, but to not acknowledge the difference based on this reality is simply ignoring the truth.

We women have a lot of "gaps."

In the United States, there has been a well-documented gender pay gap, as far back as the US Civil War. While men went off to war, women were asked to do the work previously done by men but for half the rate, if not less. These pay gaps still exist everywhere, and they are worldwide.

There's also a gender wealth gap. A recent study by investing firm Ellevest shows that women are half as likely to invest as men are, with only 30 percent of women having met with a financial planner.

In compiling research for this book, I've determined that there's another massive gap, one that is similarly preventing women from acquiring generational wealth. I've termed this the "exit gap."

When women sell their companies, they're selling them for significantly less than their male counterparts.

While I may have been the first to give this gap a name, the data has existed for decades.

A recent study completed by UK accounting firm Buzzacott looked at company exits over a ten-year period, from 2012 to 2022. The results were disheartening.

Over those ten years, less than 1 percent of businesses that sold a majority stake were female founded.

Yes, you read that correctly. That average number comes from US businesses (1.37 percent) and businesses throughout Europe and the rest of the world, which stood at 0.35 percent each.

There are two areas where female-founded companies are most prevalent: Technology, Media, and Communications (TMT) and Consumer Products. For the consumer products sector, male-founded companies sold for 18 percent higher. For TMT the disparity was even worse. The average transaction value of male-founded exits within technology, media, and communications was 1.5 times greater than female-founded equivalents.

But hey, that's just one study out of an accounting firm in London, looking at a few sectors. It's too narrow, right? Let's turn to Pitchbook, the go-to reporting source on company exits.

Pitchbook looked at VC exits and tracked exit value by the gender of the company founders.

As of 2022, all female-founded companies were capturing just 0.8 percent of exit value as of 2022.

I know, you're befuddled right now. *Carrie,* you're thinking to yourself, *you mean to tell me that for every dollar that's spent on buying a company, female founders are capturing less than a penny? How is this possible?*

Well, my friend, it is real, and it is very upsetting. But when I see a problem like this, first I seek to understand why it exists. And then, I get to work.

Why *does* this exist?

It's certainly not from a lack of women starting businesses; 2024's Impact of Women-Owned Businesses report by Wells Fargo showed that women-owned businesses are opening at twice the rate of population growth consecutively for the past five years. There are 14 million women-owned businesses in existence in the United States as of this writing.

We are starting businesses. What is holding us back from growing them into sellable assets? Let's ruminate together.

The quick answer that people love to point to is the giant gap in venture capital allocated to men versus women. Women currently capture just over 2 percent of investment funding. But let's step back for a second, because this isn't only happening in Silicon Valley, where funds are needed to "be the next Mark Zuckerberg." These growth numbers and the disparity between men- and women-owned businesses are as evident on Main Street as they are in modern-day tech firms.

Yes, funding problems affect Main Street businesses, too. When you're building a business on Main Street, you're not seeking investment dollars. You might, however, try to get a bank loan. According to a study done through Tayne Law Group, men are three times more likely to get a business loan than women. Their study found that, pre-pandemic, 85 percent of men surveyed received a small business loan, while only 36 percent of women were approved.

But you and I both know it's not just lack of funds that keeps us from thinking about growth.

Of course, there's that pesky old pressure of caretaking. Whether it's caring for children, parents, or partners, family obligations are a reality for many women. It's hard to think about scaling when you're juggling the responsibilities of caring for everyone around you.

Perhaps we're just focused on surviving. Nearly three-quarters (72 percent) of women started their businesses out of a desire to increase their money in their hands *today*. Maybe they're not focused on building something splashy, but they're focused on something substantive that can help pay the bills for their household. One of my favorite sayings in business goes, "Revenue is vanity, profit is sanity." We cannot afford to not be sane, which throws risk-taking in pursuit of revenue right out the window.

All of those pressures, combined with our desire for practicality, make building a company to "exit" feel like an unrelatable, unattainable pipe dream. (But fear not, my dear female founders: it's not!)

By the way, let's say you *do* finally get to a place where you are ready to exit. Chances are that when you are sitting at the deal table, you will be surrounded mostly by male decisionmakers. According to research from McKinsey, as a collective, PE firms manage over $10 trillion in assets, but women make up only 12 percent of managing directors and 16 percent of partners in investment roles. This is often who you're sitting across from when selling a business.

So believe me, I get it when women tell me they're keeping their heads down and scrappily building the businesses they can, as best they can, trying to stay afloat.

But make no mistake, that means we are building lifestyle businesses that likely will live and die with us, perhaps providing us with money to live well enough, with no wealth beyond the income we generate in the right-now.

I am here to tell you that it doesn't have to be that way. This data may seem scary, but if you ask me, I think the main reason we are starting businesses at a record pace but selling businesses at a snail's pace is because we simply don't realize it's possible.

I am here to tell you that it's possible.

I am here to *show* you that it's possible!

I am here to show you that you can build a lifestyle business at your own pace, or you can go big and try to build something substantial, and that *either way*, you deserve to extract the value of your business when it's time to exit.

I'm a bootstrapped entrepreneur who exited my business and learned a lot along the way. I'm a podcaster who has interviewed over two hundred female entrepreneurs about their journeys from scale through sale. And I'm committed to helping you turn your lifestyle business into a **life-changing asset**.

Seventy-five percent of business owners (regardless of gender) plan to sell their company in the next ten years. Which means there are a lot of women out there who could use a guide for how to make sure they get as much at exit as possible.

How can we build businesses that make us more money? How can we exit those businesses on our own terms, extracting life-changing value?

A recent *Inc.* article reported that 48 percent of female founders cite a lack of available mentors as a significant challenge. I hope you consider this book as your collective of mentors. I hope you find women whom you can relate to, who spark joy, motivate you, and inspire you to take decisive actions.

Oh, right, about the book!

This book is centered around a fable—a story of nine women coming together to solve their biggest business and life challenges using a method I created, called the Whisper Way. The Whisper Way is a methodology for managing, scaling, and ultimately selling your business, and I introduce it to you through a story that can be enjoyed as if it were a good beach read. I've read hundreds of business books over the course of my career, and I've written two now, and I can tell you that the ones I found the most memorable contained a story that flowed, that I could relate to, and that drew me in. This is that story, and I hope you find your own within its pages.

The women in the stories, and the businesses they own, are fictional, but I like to think that there's a little bit of us in all of them. Any similarities you find to women you know are coincidental, but not unexpected, since the characters experience so many of the same emotions we all live on a daily basis as entrepreneurs.

Actually, that's not entirely true.

The main character of this book is named Ramona, and I loaned her my Whisper Way methodology so that she can be the first to share it with you. Ramona is an exited founder who is sort of woo-woo, living in the woods. She clasps her hands in prayer. She is all things beautiful and joyous, and she is a real help to the women in this book. While Ramona isn't entirely based on me, she is exactly who I would be if pesky old reality didn't get in the way. I don't live in the woods. I don't wear caftans. I am not really all that calm, cool, and collected. But boy, I wish I were. I simply took the aspirational parts of myself and poured them into this woman. Maybe one day, I will really be Ramona, but until I am, I can't wait for you to meet her in the pages of this book.

While the characters are fictional, I've included a real-life example at the end of many chapters, showing you the story of a woman who scaled her business. To quote children's rights activist and author Marian Wright Edelman, "You can't be what you can't see," and I felt that including real-life examples beyond my own experience was essential. For each step of the Whisper Way methodology, I've also included a thought-starter exercise for you to think about the section and how you might apply it to your own business.

While much of the book is about other women and how the lessons they learn might apply to you, the last chapter is *all* about you. It's an implementation guide for the Whisper Way, which shows you how to build your own Whisper Way plan and set yourself on a course to turn your lifestyle business into a life-changing asset.

Speaking of the Whisper Way—my next company is called The Whisper Group, and we offer strategic planning and exit planning services for women-owned businesses. This book is my gift to you, and it contains a lot of my own secret sauce in the company I've built. Whether you build your Whisper Way on your own, or you use a Whisper Group guide to help you, I am here with you for the ride, cheering you on the entire way.

Chapter One
The Invitation

Who the hell has time for this shit?"

Elena opened the elaborate wooden box that had arrived on her doorstep by tearing off the ribbon and ripping it from its side, not realizing that the opening itself was meant to be an experience. Inside was some carefully placed greenery, with an embossed invitation on what looked like parchment paper.

Elena,

You are cordially invited . . .

. . . . . .

"Casey! Get in here! How cool is *this?*"

When her daughter, Casey, had arrived home that weekend from college, Renee thought that that would be the highlight of her week. Renee held the paper in her hands as she read the invitation aloud:

"*. . . to the first annual Whisper in the Woods . . .*"

● ● ● ● ● ●

"This is some serious 'girl power' energy right here, and I am not sure it's real."

Hannah held the parchment between her fingers and sniffed the foliage that seemed to overflow out of the box in Insta-worthy fashion. It definitely was sprayed with some smelly stuff. She thought to herself, *This can't be real.*

". . . *a carefully curated collective of women who have a unique opportunity . . .*"

● ● ● ● ● ●

"This. Is. A. Sign."

Ivy was tired. Bone tired. But she knew she had to do something to keep her agency going and growing. She'd been a big believer in signs. And so, when the box arrived on her doorstep, that's exactly how she'd interpreted it.

". . . *to turn their lifestyle businesses into life-changing assets.*"

● ● ● ● ● ●

"Oh, hell yes."

Phoebe snapped a photo of the invite and immediately posted it to Instagram. She assumed that she'd received it because her following had been growing across platforms. She captioned it: "Women need to stick together. This is what being a #badass is." She saved the post in her drafts and waited for the exact right moment to post it, since she had posted something else approximately thirty seconds earlier.

"*You've each been selected for a specific reason . . .*"

......

"Can I really make time for this?"

Sophia's son wailed in the background while her daughter donned a bucket on her head and ran aimlessly in circles. Sophia had been staring at the Whole Foods app, where she saw a product that looked almost exactly like her own. Anxiety washed over her as she picked up her son to soothe him, and calmly removed the bucket from her daughter's head.

"... *and we can guarantee that this two-night getaway will be a game changer for you and your business.*"

......

"I actually have no idea what I want to do, and that is freaking terrifying."

At forty-three years old, Wendy thought she knew herself. She was, by all accounts, successful, having exited her first business a few years back, and built a second business that had great potential. On some days, it felt like the business could be a rocket ship, and on other days, it felt like she was wasting her time. She would go from feeling like she wanted to become the next unicorn founder to feeling like she wanted to shut it all down and retire. Weren't your forties the time where you were supposed to know yourself? Wendy felt more confused than ever, and she didn't know if attending this thing would be helpful, or just remind her that she had absolutely no idea what she was doing.

"*See you there.*"

......

The invitation went out to just seven women, complete with a detailed description of the event. The Whisper in the Woods would be a three-day, two-night event, where seven entrepreneurs would workshop how to scale their businesses, allowing them more money, time, and flexibility than any of them had ever dreamed. Through something called "the Whisper Way," these women would learn from those who came before them—women who scaled and exited their businesses—and be given the tools to do what millions of men, but so few women, have done before.

While these women didn't know exactly what the event would entail based on the invitation, there was one thing, or person, that they did know. The invitation came from Ramona Kalman. Anyone who had ever read *Inc.*, *Forbes*, or *Fast Company* knew this woman's name. She'd built one of the largest independent marketing agency networks in the world and was a total media darling. After selling the network, she promptly disappeared from the public eye. And yet suddenly, here she was, sending scented invitations to seven seemingly random women business owners.

It was 8 AM when Ramona walked barefoot through the grass to her mailbox. It was quite the trek, as her land was pretty vast, but she loved the feel of the tall grass against her ankles. This would be her first Whisper in the Woods retreat at the farm, and the women would be her first guests since she'd renovated the property as a retreat space. She hoped that the business owners she'd picked were ready to get real. She had carefully curated the list of women to invite to this retreat, intentionally selecting a diverse group in every way possible. She wasn't interested in simply selecting influencers; she wanted a mix of women, from different backgrounds and industries. She had researched businesses and their founders from various groups like Entrepreneurs' Organization, Women Presidents Organization, Female Founder Collective, and more. She'd focused on their backgrounds, ages, stages of business, and their stories. But she really hoped

You are cordially invited to
the first annual Whisper in
the Woods, a carefully curated
collective of women who have
a unique opportunity to turn
their lifestyle businesses into
life-changing assets. You've
each been selected for a specific
reason, and we can guarantee
that this two-night getaway will
be a game changer for you and
your business. See you there.

that she'd picked the right women, and that, if they even showed up, the chemistry would be right.

As Ramona herself knew, the only way to get what you want is to truly know what you want. And if she could give these women the opportunity to figure out what they wanted and how to get it . . . well, that would be more rewarding than the moment the *New York Times* broke the story that she had sold her company. More rewarding even than when she plopped down a check to purchase this property in cash back in 2019.

As she approached the mailbox, doubts flickered through her mind. What if this was stupid? What if she wasn't qualified to do this? What if she couldn't help these women, and what if she wasted their time? And then, her deepest, darkest fear seeped in: What if she was a one-hit wonder and this retreat was the start of a string of epic failures?

Ramona took a deep breath. Instead of pushing away the fears, she focused on feeling them. Every inhale came with a question of her own self-worth. Every exhale sent them flying away. She kept going until there was no more doubt. There was only one foot, placed in front of the other, walking toward the mailbox, which would hold the answer to what happens next.

Right there at the mailbox, Ramona opened all seven RSVP cards, each bearing a little signal about the woman who'd sent it. Renee had added a +1 (well, Ramona supposed that would be fine). Sophia's was stained ("Sorry," she'd written, "Jack got his carrots on this."). Phoebe had added her Instagram handle. Only Wendy had declined, but then crossed that out. Seven "accepts" stared back at her.

Ramona smiled. In truth, she'd known all along what they would say.

Chapter Two

Welcome

Ramona's retreat was not exactly an easy place to find. After arriving in New York City, you had to take a long, winding road up into the Catskills. The Catskills, once the glory place of New York City summers, had become fairly decrepit—as if frozen in time back in the days of the film *Dirty Dancing*. Abandoned bungalows and empty, dilapidated hotels lined the road to Ramona's farm. But that's sort of how she wanted it. She was absolutely, positively done with the New York City scene and its glitzy summertime sidekick, the Hamptons. After years of keeping up with the Joneses, Ramona was ready to live a simpler life, away from the need to show everyone up. It was ironic that, now, she technically would be one of the richest self-made women on the Upper East Side, and instead she was watching seven cars slowly trek up her long, winding dirt road in the middle of nowhere.

"Welcome! Welcome!" Ramona stood there, in her gauzy print caftan, welcoming eight women into her arts and crafts living room. Exposed wooden beams layered across the ceiling like a lofted grid,

7

and eight patterned cushions were positioned perfectly in a circle around a large coffee table. The room smelled like a pleasant combination of lavender and fresh paint.

The women gazed around them as they entered the space. Hannah thought this might be a re-creation of that show *Nine Perfect Strangers*, where Nicole Kidman hosts a wackadoo wellness retreat and tortures her guests. Or some kind of real-life version of a Jordan Peele film. But she believed in her business, and she was committed to building something meaningful, so she reminded herself to stay open.

Renee looked around in awe. This was the exact type of property she'd buy if she ever could. She stared at Ramona, who looked like she was wearing little to no makeup, and seemed effortless in every way. She grasped Casey's hand, and she felt that, even if she herself wasn't a big enough deal to be here, her daughter could accomplish just about anything. She was so grateful to give her the opportunity to do so.

Elena was the last to walk in, and bumped into one of the garden stools that was serving as a small side table, probably because she was looking at her phone. She was furiously texting her client, whose daughter had just been rejected on her Early Decision application to Brown University.

"Early Decision isn't our end game. Don't worry. We have so many options," she texted. She put her phone on airplane mode and promised herself she would keep it that way, at least until her four o'clock call.

"Okay, ladies, let's have a seat," Ramona said and gestured toward the cushions. "It's time to get started."

The eight women lowered themselves onto the cushions, smiling at each other as they got settled.

"First, I want to introduce myself," Ramona said, her hands clasped in some sort of namaste-type fashion. "I am Ramona Kalman.

I built and sold one of the largest independent creative agencies in the country. Scaling and selling that business was one of the most joyful, terrifying, overwhelming, and meaningful experiences of my life. It involved stories of success and of struggle. Our company's work won countless Cannes Lions awards . . . and we almost missed payroll on several occasions. There were so many times where I questioned myself, my own worth, my agency's worth. Other times I was convinced I was the toughest leader you've ever met and could accomplish anything I set my mind to. And when I finally sold the company that I dedicated my life to, I sat across from men, negotiating as the only woman in the room, for the largest transaction of my life.

"After I sold, I really had to reexamine my identity, and my purpose—and you, my friends, you are the start of that next journey for me. I am here to help you do what I did, which is to grow your companies to a place where you can have the life you want. I don't care if you want to sell. I don't care if you want to stay small, but build your business so that you can live the life you want, on your own terms. What I want for you is to *know* what you want, and to set a plan to help you get there. And what I want is for each of you to understand that these incredible, awe-inspiring lifestyle businesses you created—they're not just that alone. These are *assets*—assets that can change your life, as long as you are willing to get honest, get clear, and get focused."

She saw Hannah shift in her seat. Ramona started internally panicking. *Are they into this? Speed it up, lady,* she thought to herself. *You don't want to lose them.*

"I created a methodology called the Whisper Way. It's a system for women to scale their businesses to be sale ready, if they should ever choose to do so. It's designed to help you have more control over your money, and your time. It's different from other methods for two reasons. First, it tackles the emotions behind your motivations and your actions. And second, this system is designed for women, by a woman. Let's talk about that for a minute, if you'll bear with me."

Elena coughed. And there was Ramona's inner voice again, telling her to get to the point. *Shut up, inner critic. I'm in the zone.* She continued, but vowed to wrap up quickly.

"Did you know that women-owned businesses are growing at *twice* the rate of the population? Impressive, right? Sure, except when you look at the revenue numbers. Companies that are owned by men are earning double the amount of what female businesses earn.

"Listen, there's a million reasons why that could be. But if you ask me personally, I think it's that women start businesses for different reasons than men. Maybe we want to be able to have control over our time, to have the ability to be at our daughter's soccer game at three o'clock on a Thursday. Maybe it's because we experienced rampant sexism at work. Maybe it's because we are afraid of taking risks since so many of us are bootstrapping these businesses—either because we can't get the funding, or because we build businesses that require less startup capital because we have to, and because, dammit, if we were going to take a bet on anyone, it is going to be on ourselves. That's how I started, selling logos at two hundred bucks a pop because I knew I could. And then suddenly, I had ten employees. Do you know *how* many women call themselves 'accidental entrepreneurs'? A lot. Most of us don't start with our chests puffed out, thinking we are going to be Elon Musk. And listen, hurray for us if we do. But I know I certainly didn't, and the hundreds of women business owners I've spoken to over the years didn't either."

Ivy felt the air leave her lungs as she listened to Ramona. It was like someone finally understood what her journey was like. Ramona picked up on the change of energy in the room and decided to run with it. She continued—she was on a roll, and neither Ivy nor the other women in the room could take their eyes off of her.

"You know, when I was starting the idea for this new business, I had a lot of fear. I had never worked in finance, or mergers and acquisitions, or even consulting. But you know when I knew that I had to do this? There were two moments, actually. The first was when I spoke to a man who built a membership program—a collective of agencies that he would help to scale and sell. It was exactly what I originally wanted to build, but mine would be exclusively for women. I was asking him for feedback, and maybe thinking we could do some sort of partnership—I really was just exploring. And he said to me, clear as day, 'You know, I don't think the M&A experience is any different for a woman than it is for a man.'"

"*Pffft*," said Phoebe. "Spoken like a *man*."

The ladies chuckled. Casey clapped.

"That same day," said Ramona, "I attended a networking dinner for M&A professionals and met some private equity guys, some advisors, and some heads of some pretty big law firms. I explained to this one advisor what I was trying to do. And I remember he looked at me like I was pretty naive. He said, 'Oh, that's going to be hard. PE for example doesn't like to acquire women- or minority-owned businesses—since, once acquired, they lose their status as a woman-owned business.'"

"That's really true?" said Sophia. She looked like she was going to cry. Private equity was where she had set her sights, just as soon as WholeHeart had enough distribution to warrant it.

"I don't know if it's always true, but I do know that this is the type of stuff that's said in rooms that most of us never have access to. And I know that it's time that this changes. That's why I've started The Whisper Group, and it launches right now with all of you.

"We're going to start with intros, and an assessment which you'll all take. After that we will workshop each of your businesses, all of which, from my initial research, need help in one area of the Whisper Way. You will leave here with a plan and a path to achieve what you want, in the timeline you want it."

A soft voice rose up from the impeccably dressed woman seated in the seat farthest from Ramona. "What if we truly don't know what we want?"

"Well, Wendy," said Ramona, in the most calming of tones, "that's exactly why you're here. Now let's get started."

As Ramona phased everyone into the introductions part of the day, a collective energy buzzed through the room. Something was happening, even if they all were unsure of exactly what.

"As we begin," said Ramona, "I want to know your name and where you're from. I want to know about your business, and any backstory you think is important about that business, while keeping it tight—there are a lot of you! Oh, and one more thing I want you to answer. Tell me about your relationship with money."

The room fell silent.

"Oh, we're really doing this now?" said Hannah. Despite her initial concerns, Ramona's speech resonated with her. If she was here, she might as well lean in. "All right, I'll go first."

As she stood, everyone shifted on their cushions to look at Hannah. She was absolutely gorgeous, even in the modest athleisure and sneakers she'd worn.

"Hey everyone, I'm Hannah. I'm the founder of OurHour, which is a fitness program that I recently launched an app for. I was a Soul-Cycle instructor for years, and I built up quite a following. But honestly, it held no meaning for me. These ladies shelled out $50 per *class* to watch me empower them, scream in their faces, and then end with some candles and some namaste-ness, and it just felt like I was on a perpetual episode of *The Real Housewives of Beverly Hills*, which makes sense because that is where I taught over in West Hollywood. I really wanted to democratize fitness, and to bring it to members of my community—folks who were not spending fifty bucks on a forty-five-minute class that came with some free Boxed Water. I started with hosting outdoor classes in Hyde Park with a 'pay what you can' model. I focused on creating a unique class—a mix of cardio, yoga, and meditation, designed to have you leave feeling totally fulfilled. I stayed at SoulCycle too, until I started making enough from the classes to leave.

"I've been intent on scaling this beyond the park, and so I raised I guess what would be called an 'angel round'—by which I mean begging my friends and family for money—and built an app that replicates my classes in a scalable way. I raised $75,000 to do it, and I could not believe my community showed up for me in that way. So, while it was being built, I was really excited. And now that it's here, I have no idea how the heck to get anyone outside of my own community to use it. And I'm just feeling like maybe I should have stuck to keeping this shit in the park, you know what I mean? I feel paralyzed.

"In terms of my feelings about money? Well, I grew up safe, secure, and smack in the middle of the middle class. My parents both worked for the government and built a secure life that was not based on any form of risk. So where the hell did I come from, building this app? I didn't do a real fundraising round because if you think the stats are shitty for women, try being a Black woman with a limited network. But I *did* raise from my community, which to me is infinitely more pressure than raising money from some rich investors. These are people I see every day. The thought of letting them down keeps me up at night. So money for me is less about me personally. I'm thirty years old, I'm single, and I don't need much. But I can't let down the people who invested in me, *and* I want to build something that doesn't cost people an arm and a leg just to sweat with a bunch of other rich skinny bitches, you know? And honestly, I'm scared there's not a place for a business like mine, and that I'm going to have to look people I know and love in the face and say, 'You made a bad bet.'"

As Hannah sat down, everyone stared at her. Her story made sense—she had the glow of someone who truly emanated goodness from their soul.

"Wow," said Renee. "You are an inspiration, Hannah. I'm so happy that my daughter is here to see you—and I have no doubt that you'll shine. I guess I'll go next."

Renee fiddled with her patterned blouse as she took a deep breath. "Hi, I'm Renee, and this is my daughter, Caaaaasey." She elongated her daughter's name as if it was a warm cup of tea being stirred with love. It was clear that she adored her, and the women in the room all collectively smiled at the introduction.

"I was born and raised in Omaha. About twenty years ago, when Casey was two years old, I opened Coffee+, a small coffee shop located downtown. It's been lovely, really, and Coffee+ is like having another child. I've been running it pretty well, I'd say, and the income from the shop allowed us to have a good life. I was able to send Casey to school with no loans, which is something I'm really proud of, and I paid off our mortgage last year. One of the things I'm proudest of with Coffee+ is that it's become the de facto hangout spot for the community. Folks co-work there all the time, and I do have a good group of regulars. And it's all fine . . . just fine. But recently, I saw that yet another Starbucks was opening in town. Except this time, it's right down the street. Oh, not just a regular one, either, it's a drive-through that has a big communal space in the shop, too.

"Gosh, maybe if I was younger, I'd have the guts to do some kind of smart marketing campaign or something, but I just really think it might be time for me to throw in the towel and close up shop. I know Casey has some big ideas, but I don't want to burden her with a business that requires you to be there all the time, and especially when times are changing.

"In terms of my feelings about money? Well, I've always been pretty frugal and have been very hesitant about debt. I guess I just never wanted to owe anything to anyone. Maybe that's why I started this in the first place. If I succeeded or if I failed, it was on me."

"Hey, Mom?" Casey took her mother's hand, which was still twisting the corner of her blouse. "Can I share what I see when I look at your story?"

"Of course," said Renee.

"My mom has run this shop since before I can remember. Now that I'm older, I see how opening it *was* a risk. My dad didn't make a ton of money as a truck driver, and he was gone a lot. After the accident, my mother was completely on her own with me. She worked around the clock to build a life for me, and for us. She doesn't deserve to be run out of business, just because someone decided that a Starbucks belongs on the same block as us. She also should consider taking some chances. Her coffee is damn good, and so are her baked goods. Why shouldn't she, why couldn't *we*, think about leaning in versus stepping out, especially at a time where we feel financially stable?"

"Because," said Renee, "we've worked hard for all of this, and I couldn't possibly bear to put you in any position that could potentially hurt our security."

"But, Mom," said Casey softly, "we *are* safe. We *are* secure. And what's life without taking a chance or two?"

Renee leaned her head on Casey's shoulder. "I told y'all she was a good kid."

"Wow," said Phoebe. "You guys are lucky. Security is a pipe dream for me."

Like Hannah, Phoebe stood up to speak. She was dressed in all black, with tons of rings and bracelets, an eclectic mix of pieces that all just seemed to work.

"I'm Phoebe, and I'm from New York City. You may recognize me from my TikToks. Honestly, I'm pretty well known from that at this point. I took out a shit ton of loans to go to Emerson College, where I majored in Writing, Literature, and Publishing. I started recording my spoken word poetry on TikTok, and when one piece that I wrote about the crushing weight of student loans exploded, I decided that I would start creating content for Gen Z women artists making their way through the education system. I began getting so many comments from women like me, women who were trying to make their way through the start of their career as artists. Two years after graduation, I decided to start Be A Badass Inc., a membership collective for young women who were looking for peer groups and guidance monetizing their art. I've had *so* much interest, and my newsletter sign-ups are through the roof, but getting these women to actually pay has proven to be more difficult than I initially thought. My monthly paying memberships are growing, but slowly, and people cancel frequently. Today, I'm making most of my money through my own content creation as a TikTok influencer, but it's not much.

"So how do I feel about money? Well, I live in New York City, where the cost of a latte is probably a lot more than you charge in Omaha, Renee."

Renee nodded and yelled out, "Amen, ain't that the truth!"

"Look, I'm young. I'm an artist. I don't need much to live, and trust me, as an influencer, you can basically live off of product that's sent to you on the regular. But I have student loans looming over my head, and of course, I'd be lying if I said I didn't want to make Be A Badass something huge that makes tons of money. So I guess the answer is, I need money, I like money. I'm a badass who plans to make a shit ton of money. But right now? Your girl is straight-up broke. But in some ways, having nothing makes me more fearless, right? When you've got nothing, you've got nothing to lose."

"You've got a lot more than nothing, Phoebe! You've got *freedom*! I don't even know how I managed to extricate myself today to get here." A quieter, but firm voice rose from the opposite corner of the circle. She suspected she'd never quite have the type of fearlessness that Phoebe had, so there was no point in waiting any longer to speak. All she had was her own story, and that would have to be good enough.

"The first thing I'm going to tell you is that I'm sort of embarrassed by my privilege," said Sophia. "But I feel like I'm holding it together by a thread." Sophia looked like the type of person who tried to present an air of perfection, but you could immediately spot her reality. Her hair was pulled back into a tight bun, except for one imperfect bump at the top of her hair. She wore a white button-down with linen pants, which seemed to have at least two coffee stains on them. And behind very well-applied makeup that showed off that coveted "dewy glow," the bags under her eyes still showed just how tired she was.

"My name is Sophia, I'm thirty-six years old, I live just outside of Denver. My husband, Greg, is a lawyer, and we have three amazing kids, Vivian, who is five, Cole, who is three, and Jack, who just turned one. I am the owner of WholeHeart—"

"Oh, shit! I love WholeHeart! The bite-sized, heart-shaped organic chocolates in Whole Foods?" Hannah broke in.

"Yep, those are the ones!" Sophia said proudly, then continued. "I truly was, the way Ramona described it, an accidental entrepreneur. I never intended to work. I had the kids. My husband has a secure job. But when Vivi started going out into the world, I got really freaked out about the toxins in our everyday foods. I started home cooking *everything*. Monitoring every ingredient. I became kind of obsessive. As she got older and Cole came along, I started trying to make food, especially organic food, fun. I created these little heart-shaped nuggets— think Hershey kisses but healthy and in the shape of a heart. And I filled them with the most delicious creamy filling. They loved it. My husband loved it. Everyone at every playdate was obsessed.

"That was when Greg started encouraging me to sell at farmers markets. I wasn't even sure if I'd have the time, and also, I wanted a third baby. But I started selling on Saturdays and sold out immediately, every week. It was really rewarding to me.

"I went to Vivi's preschool orientation, and I brought some snacks. If I told you what happened next, you wouldn't believe me. The *buyer for our region of Whole Foods* is a mom at school. I brought snacks, and the next thing you know, I'm in at Whole Foods, I'm in at Safeway. Natural Grocers! My husband helped us take in some funding—I think it was a loan?—and we started working with a distributor.

"I really felt like this was my calling. Managing it all while having Jack and raising the two bigs is tough, but it was exciting."

"This sounds like a straight-up badass fairy tale, good for you!" Phoebe nodded enthusiastically. This was exactly what she came here to see. Women who were winning the game.

"Sure," said Sophia. "But now I'm in the supposed *big leagues*. And I'm walking down the aisle at Whole Foods, and I see them: a *complete* rip-off of my product. Same design, similar packaging, and a lower price. I felt like I couldn't breathe, like my perfect vision was getting stomped on. And now, my orders continue to rise, which requires more funding. My kids continue to need me, which requires more time and energy. And I'm no longer unique or special? It's too much to bear.

"In terms of money, I grew up with it, and don't think about it too much. I'm lucky to have a husband I can count on in this way. But the idea that I'm going to suddenly invest a ton in a business that can be easily replicated? For what? I don't know that I have it in me to be this competitive shark, and I don't know exactly why my product is better than anyone else's, and I'm afraid now that maybe we'll go deep into debt for a dream that was simply an accident."

Sophia realized that she was starting to cry, and quickly composed herself, her mascara smearing just enough to be visible to the highly trained eye of another mother who was completely exhausted.

Ivy got up from her cushion and snuck next to Sophia, putting her hand over hers. "I totally get it, Sophia. I really do."

Ivy felt so energized being surrounded by these women, each with their own experiences and stories. They were all doing the damn thing, under what felt like impossible circumstances.

"Hi, I'm Ivy, I'm from Boston, and I am the CEO and founder of Major Makers, a creative agency that specializes in storytelling. I have an eight-year-old son and a two-year-old daughter, and I started the business six years ago. I worked at a creative agency for years until I felt like I couldn't take the hours. I was getting home past my son's bedtime and that was just not what I wanted out of life. I started freelancing as a creative director, but I found that positioning myself as a freelancer got me smaller jobs. So I created Major Makers, which was really just me and a few contract workers. But I think because I positioned it as an agency, we were seen as bigger than we actually were. When we were featured in *Adweek* for our digital storytelling work with a startup, the calls started coming in, and I landed my first *Fortune* 500 client. That led to lots of hiring. So now, cash is more of an issue. And, more than that, the client? They are very demanding because they can be. Forty of my fifty people work on this client, and I wake up in a sweat each night thinking they're going to fire us.

"Because I worked like a dog at an agency when I was younger, I really don't want the same for my people. I want them to have work-life balance; I want them to have a quality of life. But when this client struggles, we all struggle.

"Also, I want to point out that I'm weird with money. When I was working as an employee, I never really felt any issues. And honestly, I think throughout most of my early days, I was scared but not terrified. But now? Now that I have this payroll and I'm this big and my family is used to the lifestyle this agency brings us? I really feel like at any moment it could all go away and I'll be homeless!"

As soon as it came out of her mouth, Ivy felt like she sounded like a moron. Who has a fifty-person agency and is afraid of being homeless? But when she looked around the room, she saw faces that were empathetic and understanding. She saw her people.

"Thanks for letting me share that, you guys. I feel a little stupid."

"You are not stupid, Ivy," said Elena. "You're captivating. Honestly, I didn't want to look down at my phone once while you were talking."

Elena spoke at a fast pace, and she used exactly zero unnecessary words.

"I'm Elena. I'm from Bethesda, Maryland. I'm forty years old. I run Wise Words College Prep."

She took a short breath, calculating in her mind how quickly she could speak in order to get them moving along to the next part of this exercise. Because Elena needed help.

"I was the director of admissions at a private high school. Connected with the kids really well, and eventually helped them with their college applications as a side gig. I got my kids in everywhere. Harvard, USC, you name it. I helped with essays primarily. I liked the extra income; it worked for me. Eventually, I got tired of my job, but I am not ever going back to being someone without money. I'm forty years old. I don't have a lot of earning years left, and my job got boring, so I decided to hustle. I saved a year's worth of my salary and put it in an LLC and opened Wise Words. I figured I'd give it a year. Within a year, I was already making double what I made at the private school. I make a lot of money. I save a lot of money. I spend a lot of money. I like money, and I'm not embarrassed by that. I've made more than any other family member in my life. I am not married. I have no kids. This is my identity, and I like it that way. I won't apologize for it."

Elena's phone buzzed.

"Oh my goodness, I'm so sorry, you guys, I have to take this."

And with that, Elena stepped out of the room, leaving the door slightly ajar.

The mouths in the room were mostly agape. Hannah wasn't sure if she was impressed or disgusted. Phoebe? Definitely loving it. Felt like major "girlboss" energy.

Ramona could hear Elena's side of the phone call, where she calmly explained the difference between an Early Acceptance application and an Early Decision. It seemed unfathomable to Ramona that Elena would disrespect the first session like this, and she hoped she hadn't made the wrong choice in selecting her. Just as Ramona was about to approach her, Elena scurried back into the room. She was clearly flustered.

"I don't know why I can't sit for three freaking days at this workshop without having these people call me every two minutes! I love my work, but this is not sustainable. But who the hell am I if I'm not this?"

"Ah, who the hell am I? That's the question I've been asking myself this entire time listening to all of you." Wendy wasn't ready, but she was the last one in the room, and there was no other option.

"Okay, maybe that's a bit dramatic, but when I tell you I don't know what I want, I'm not kidding."

Wendy was dressed in a silk patterned dress with a deep V-neck. Her hair looked straight out of a fresh Drybar Mai Tai blowout—and there wasn't a chipped nail to be found on her hands or her perfectly pedicured tan feet.

"I'm Wendy. Good luck getting me to tell you my age, but it's safe to say, I'm not in my twenties anymore. Ivy, we actually have something in common! I built an agency, although it was smaller than yours—a PR shop out of Miami. I sold it to Ketchum in my thirties." (She paused, realizing she had just revealed that she was no longer in her thirties, either!) "I've had a lot of lives, really. I worked the makeup counter at Bloomingdale's in my early days, then I became a personal stylist there. I loved that job. I loved knowing instantly if I was the right fit for someone as a stylist, or if they needed someone else. I was versatile, sure, but I felt like I only wanted to work with people who I really clicked with. It was fun. But then I started the fashion PR firm, and that was great too. The exit was nice, but it certainly wasn't fuck-you money, not by Miami standards anyway. But it *was* enough to keep some for myself and invest some in an idea. I built a technology that would allow people to answer a few questions about their style, and match them with a stylist in their area. It's called Fashion Faire. I make money in two ways. First, I get a cut of the stylist's revenue that comes from booking through the site.

Second, my relationships with fashion houses and retail from my PR days led to some great sponsorships and advertising. And here's the thing, you guys . . ."

Her voice started to quiver. It looked like she was smiling and crying at the same time. *How could someone look so happy and so sad all at once?* thought Renee. She wanted to give her a hug.

"This thing . . . it could be a *rocket ship*, okay? I see it. I am self-funded. I am making money. But if I want it to grow, I need more money. A lot of it. In the Miami startup scene there are so many entrepreneurs that raise funds, are pre-revenue, talk a lot of shit, and fall flat on their faces. I can't be that person. And at the same time, if I want this to succeed, do I have to swim in those circles? I vacillate constantly between running this as a small, profitable, bootstrapped business, or a *go big* funded startup that will revolutionize the ability to insert relational connection into fashion."

She stopped and looked around.

"As for money. You need a lot of it to look this good." (*They all really knew this, right? They had to,* thought Wendy.) "And oddly enough, staying small allows me the control I need to control my own income and my destiny. And plus, what if I raise money and it fails? I'd be completely humiliated and the laughingstock of the Miami startup scene."

Casey couldn't help it. She had to say something, even if she wasn't one of the "entrepreneurs" in the room. "Wendy," she said as she looked her straight in the eye. "That is a *fantastic* company idea."

Ramona stepped into the center of the circle. "That was simply wonderful. You were honest, you were real, and you shared with one another. Hopefully you see that you're not alone. Okay, the next step is to take an assessment." She pointed to a sign on the wall that featured a QR code. "Please scan the QR code on this sign. You'll be led to a series of thirty-five simple questions. You don't need anything to prep for this. Just answer quickly and honestly. There are some refreshments over in the studio—" She gestured over to another area where easels filled with colorful paintings filled the room. "Go get a snack, take a breather, and take the assessment as soon as you're ready."

Chapter Three

The Assessment

Each of the women scanned the code and began the quiz, trying to answer without thinking about it too much. There were thirty-five questions, which were, for the most part, quite simple. Some questions, though? They needed to think about more than others.

. . . . . .

Q1: I know exactly why I started this business.

Wendy was already stuck. Did she start Fashion Faire as a fun little project? Or did she start it to be the next billion-dollar female-founder-led business?

. . . . . .

Q4: We have a unique offering that our competitors simply don't match.

God, did I used to, thought Sophia. She was once so sure of Whole-Heart and its differentiator. But now, all she could picture were the competitive products on the shelf.

· · · · · ·

Q7: I am comfortable in rooms occupied mostly by older men.

This question made Renee shudder. She was comfortable in her coffee shop. Why did she *ever* think she should try and grow Coffee+, let alone compete against the likes of Starbucks?

Casey was filling it out too, just for fun. She'd never been in that sort of office setting, but she'd try anything once. Maybe she was too young to know any better, but she felt like she could stand up to every single suit on the board at any company if it meant helping her mom succeed.

· · · · · ·

Q14: I know what is needed to keep growing this business.

This question stopped Hannah dead in her tracks. She knew how to do workouts in the park. She knew how to inspire. And you'd best believe she knew how to get people in shape. But how to get people to pay for the app they downloaded? Or even download it at all? Eek.

· · · · · ·

Q18: I can accurately forecast revenue for the next year with relative ease.

Ivy was already freaking out over the question about no client representing more than 20 percent of her revenue—she had one client that probably accounted for about 70 percent of all the dollars of Major Makers. But what scared her more than that was her inability to know where new business was coming from, and how much she'd shrink or grow each year. She was focused on her staff, and the unpredictability was what kept her from feeling secure about keeping them all happy and engaged.

. . . . . .

Q24: I completely trust my executive team.

Elena stood up and paced around the room. Maybe this workshop wasn't for her. She was a solopreneur. These questions don't apply! She didn't need anyone else for Wise Words—she could rely on herself. No one could do it like she could. Plus, these questions were taking too much time and the notifications coming in from her phone kept taking her out of the app anyway. She wished there was an N/A option for some of these questions.

. . . . . .

Q35: I consider myself to be a risk taker.

Oh, hell yes, thought Phoebe. *Taking risks is my love language! I put my poetry out there, I'm a certified freaking badass, for goodness' sake!* She was feeling really good about these questions. There was just the whole issue of the "multiples," the "profitability," the business-y questions. She didn't know how to answer them. But she had to appear confident . . . so she sort of winged it through those. *Absolutely!*

. . . . . .

Q26: I can picture what my life looks like after I am done running this business.

Although all the ladies worked through the quiz at different speeds, one thing was the same for all of them when taking this quiz. All of them went back to this question to revisit it. Not one of them could quite picture what their life would look like after running their business.

27

. . . . . .

"All right, ladies! Gather around. It's time to get started!"

Ramona's voice sounded chipper, but inside she was panicking. She'd heard some of the women questioning the prompts in the assessment, which of course caused her to doubt herself. Was she even qualified to host this thing? Could she help these women? Ramona knew that confidence was as important as competence, but at this moment, she was feeling a lack of both. There was absolutely nothing to do but put one foot in front of the other, and introduce these women to the Whisper Way.

"When I said you were a carefully curated group of women, I didn't mean because you all had different backgrounds, or different businesses . . . although of course you all do. And I didn't mean that you all had different feelings about money—which you all sort of do, too. What I meant is that each of you have challenges that represent each of the seven tenets of the Whisper Way. Together, we will workshop these tenets, and hopefully, you will each learn from one another as we tackle your challenges."

Ramona took a deep breath. Here was the moment she had been waiting for. The moment that she was going to launch her own success story that was going to take her from "cool, quirky coach" to "operational systems leader" of a business that would grow to be bigger than her wildest dreams. She took a quick mental note to remember this moment and how she felt. Succeed or fail, this was the start of something big in her life, and that was exciting.

"The Whisper Group is my latest venture. It's designed to help women like you prepare their businesses for the future, and, as I said earlier, turn each of your lifestyle businesses into life-changing assets. The Whisper Group has a few promises that we make to business owners like you.

"First, we thrive on *simplicity*. We don't use jargon, or complicated terms that only someone who dropped two hundred grand on an MBA would understand. We break down complex concepts, simply. Our method is simple, our explanations are simple, and any plans you make for your business will be simple. Because most of us who start these businesses don't start them because we have a finance degree, a trust fund, and understand our CAC. That's Customer Acquisition Cost for those of you who don't know that—which is probably quite a few of you—and that's *okay*! All of that is out the window here. You'll be able to understand what we are talking about here, and if for some reason you don't, you'll feel safe enough to ask.

"Second, we keep it completely *real*. We are honest about where you are today, and where we think you can get tomorrow. And we encourage you to get real, too. By the way, most women hear 'get real,' and they think, 'Oh, we need to get realistic, and tame down our dreams.' Actually, sometimes it's the opposite. Sometimes, your fear is holding you back from the reality of what you can actually do. It is our job to truly listen to you, and then give you the real-deal look at where you can go. It will be rooted in reality, but never limited by any belief that you are not enough. And most importantly, we want you to get absolutely clear on what it is that you want, once we remove all of the external and internal voices of judgment and expectations.

"Over our next two days together, we will workshop each of the seven tenets of scaling a successful business using a method that was created through the lens of a woman, using methodologies that are not necessarily unique to women alone, but are rooted in themes that I've heard through thousands of hours of interacting with women just like you. The Whisper Way takes a look at your Why, your How, your Income, your Secret Sauce, your Profit, your Exec Team, and last but not least, your Roar factor—which is to say, how you will show up in a room full of men when it comes time to sell your business, gain financing, or do just about anything in business. Because this is our reality. And instead of getting angry about it, or hiding from it, we must simply band together and turn our collective whispers into a giant resounding *roar*."

Ramona's heart was in her throat. She didn't have time to worry about whether or not they were buying what she was selling, or her *Jerry Maguire*-esque speech. One foot. In front of the other. Again and again.

"We will be taking some time to look at your assessment scores to identify areas of opportunity. You'll also receive a report on where your businesses are today, and together, we will craft Whisper Way plans to give you a simple path forward to achieve whatever success you determine you want. These plans will be bespoke—nothing cookie cutter—and based not only on your current business's status, but on you, the founder, and what you seek."

Even Elena was paying attention now.

"Are we ready?" said Ramona. She wasn't worried if they were into this anymore—she knew that she was on to something by the eight attentive gazes holding her own. And questioning herself did nothing anyway. She had to believe her own bullshit, and remember, of course, that it wasn't bullshit at all. And she was about to prove it.

"Wendy, come to the center of the circle, please. It's time to discuss your *Why*."

WHISPER SCORE
ASSESSMENT

The full thirty-five-question Whisper Score Assessment is available for you to take on The Whisper Group's website. Not only will you be scored for each of the tenets of the Whisper Way, but you'll also find videos explaining how you can improve in each area. Visit WeAreThe WhisperGroup.com or scan the code below.

Chapter Four

What's Your Why

Wendy did as she was told and stepped into the center of the circle. She was energized by the group, but she couldn't stop her mind from going a million miles a minute.

"All right, so I'm already thinking. I've done this before when I sold my agency. I could flip this thing, but much, much bigger. First I'll do a round by going to one of the incubators local to Miami. I know a bunch of bigwig investors from my PR days. Also, I think I can still get into Young Presidents' Org—I'm *just* young enough, and those guys have a lot of money. I feel like I could be one of the 2 percent of women that raises VC funds, I just need to raise my confidence! I've got this, guys. I just have to make sure that I have complete control, I have to make sure no one is ruining this company. I built Fashion Faire my way, and I know it's going to work, and I just need to lead it my way. Okay, I've got this, I think, I just . . ."

"Can I stop you for a second?" asked Ramona. She approached Wendy with a small package in her hand. Wendy took a breath, and apprehensively accepted it.

"I'm going to ask you to do something. You don't have to do it. But I'm going to ask anyway. Would you consider taking your makeup off?" She handed her a makeup wipe.

"Why?" said Wendy.

"Because sometimes, we wear makeup to appear a certain way. And for a moment, just a moment, I would like you to appear as unfiltered, unabashedly yourself."

"Ramona, I wear makeup to feel like the best version of myself! I run a fashion tech startup, for goodness' sake!"

"I know. Humor me if you can."

Fuck it, thought Wendy. She took the makeup wipes, walked over to the mirror, and removed her makeup.

She walked back to the center of the room.

"Thank you, Wendy," said Ramona. "Now I'm going to ask you to take two full minutes just to breathe. Stand in the middle of the circle and breathe. And then I'm going to ask you some questions. But first, I want you to take two minutes to focus on your breath and become really present."

"Ramona! I am not a meditator! What is even going on?"

"I'm not asking you to meditate. I'm asking you to breathe and slow your brain for two minutes."

Wendy decided, at that exact moment, that there was no other option but to surrender to this experience. Otherwise, why *was* she really here?

Inhale for four. Hold for four. Exhale for four. Hold for four. She remembered this breathing technique from that app she once tried when she was having anxiety attacks during her first agency business's sale. If she focused on that, she could stop her mind from racing, and stop worrying about the fact that there were eight sets of eyes, all staring at her makeup-free face. She closed her eyes, thinking maybe that would help her feel more comfortable.

"Wendy," Ramona said. "You mentioned that you were clear now—you wanted to raise VC funds. Why?"

Wendy opened her eyes. "Well, I want to build a huge business."

"Why else?" Ramona pressed.

"I see a lot of businesses in Miami raising shit tons of money, and I know my concept is better. I'm already profitable, for goodness' sake!"

"Okay. That's good, Wendy. Now, why do you want to build a huge business?"

"Well, I want to make a lot of money."

"Why else?"

"I want to be known and respected for what I've done. It pisses me off that the press goes to all these guys who have raised funds when they haven't even been profitable yet."

"Excellent. Now stop and think about this. Why do you want to make a lot of money?"

"Because I believe money allows me control and power. And I want the control and the power."

"Why do you want control?"

"Because, honestly, I have confidence in what I'm building. I know it's going to work and I don't want anyone fucking it up."

"Why do you think someone would, as you say, fuck it up?"

"I guess because I see so many of these startups raise money, never make any money, and close their doors."

"Okay, now back to what you said before, about how it upsets you about the press going to the founders that get funded versus ones that actually are successful. Why does that bother you?"

"Hmm. This is a good question. I guess because it all feels fake. Actually, a lot of what I'm surrounded by feels fake. It's hard to stay grounded and rooted in the fact that I believe in this business, and that I know it can make money without all of that. Maybe it's my PR background, but I tend to think everyone is full of shit, except me."

Phoebe cleared her throat. "As the resident social media expert of the bunch, let me assure you, they are. But also remember—in the press, the socials, all of it—you're looking at someone's highlight reel, when you're living your real life behind the scenes. So of course you feel more real."

Ramona nodded, loving the group participation. She hoped that would continue. "Okay, now I have a question for you. How much money is a lot of money to you?"

"Oh, gosh. I don't even know. I love working. I will probably work until I'm eighty! But I don't want to ever feel like I'm working because I have to, only because I want to."

"And why is that? Finish this sentence: I want to be financially free in order to . . ."

"Control my life!" exclaimed Wendy.

Now Renee spoke up. "Wendy, if I may . . . I heard three things here. First, I heard that you were set on raising VC funds. But what I also heard was you want total control, you believe in your business, and most importantly, *you're a software company* that's already making money! Honey, I own a coffee shop. I don't know the PR and finance worlds. But when I look at you, I see someone who can do this on her own."

Hannah chimed in next. "*Exactly.* And you know what else I heard, Wendy? You love the 'scene,' but you also know what it is—which is primarily bullshit. I may not swim in the Miami startup circles, but I do inspire many a woman at the West Hollywood Soul-Cycle, which is the epicenter of all things fake. You are the real deal, my friend."

"You know what I liked about that exercise?" said Elena. "I like that, when you ask the why behind the why, you avoid the Miss America answer. You know, saying you want to start a business to change the world, or help your employees, or whatever. We have been trained to have nice-girl answers—so trained, in fact, that they feel totally real. And for some of us, they are. Like Hannah, I know you want to help your community, and Ivy, I know you care about your employees. But drilling down further and asking *why* you do helps you get clearer about your goals. And to me, Wendy, I identify with your need to have control over your destiny. My problems are different. But my *why*? It's kind of similar. And I love that."

"Well," said Ramona, "we're not done here. Wendy, it's time for a tough question. When you say you want to make a lot of money, I want you to think about what that actually means to you. Because that answer is different for everyone. And this is a judgment-free space, okay? I want to know a number, or a range, or something."

God, did Wendy hate discussing money. In Miami, people were dripping in it. Boats, houses on the water, and she didn't even want to get started on the fashion.

"I feel stupid saying this. I am a single woman with no kids. To live the way I live in Miami, I still need to make about 300K a year in income. Do you guys think that's insane?"

Wendy felt so exposed giving these bigger numbers, especially since there were people in this room who probably felt that type of money for a woman with no kids was ridiculous. But it was her truth. She continued.

"That allows me to save for retirement and live the life I want. And I'm . . ." Here she paused, debating whether or not she should give her real age. Her mother was probably the only person alive who knew it! She went for it. ". . . forty-three years old. So let's say I live to ninety. I did meet with a financial planner and he had me retiring comfortably at seventy based on my retirement plan today. I split the proceeds from my first business between funding this one and my retirement money. So I guess I'd say in order to never have to work again, I'd need to fill the 300K gap for twenty-seven years if I sold today . . . so roughly . . ."

"*Eight point one million dollars!*" yelled Casey so loudly that she surprised herself. She looked around sheepishly. "I just got my degree in finance, guys, I'm trying to put it to use." Renee looked at her with such pride. Casey continued, "Wendy, imagine you sold for that much, *and* you kept working because you wanted to, not because you had to. You'd be chilling on a boat off the coast of Miami in a caftan living your best life!"

Wendy laughed and they all started chatting about Wendy's new life on her boat.

Ramona clapped her hands and brought them all back to the point. "Wendy, if you are already making revenue, taking in VC money may seem appealing, but comes at a cost to that goal. You have already self-funded the business, and if you can continue to do so, you will keep 100 percent of the sale proceeds, minus fees. If you raise money, you will be able to grow faster, but you'll need to sell for that much more to get the money you want at exit. And, what is probably most important? You will have to surrender at least some control. If you're okay with that."

"You probably won't be on the cover of the *Miami Herald*, though. Can you live with that?" asked Ivy.

Sophia joined the conversation. She'd been thinking about Wendy's child-free, seemingly carefree life and what her future might hold. "You'll shed tears of sadness whilst sunbathing on your yacht, Wendy. And you'll control which way it sails."

For the first time in a long time, Wendy felt seen.

"All right, ladies, now it's time for a group exercise. We are going to help you all work through your *why*."

Ramona distributed artfully branded, high-quality notebooks to each of the women. Even Casey got one.

"Open your notebooks and reserve three pages. On the first page I want you to write at the top: *Why did I start this business?* Then, I want you to turn to the second page. And I want you to write at the top what you think you want to do with this business. Maybe that's: *I want to sell it for ten million dollars!* Or, it could be: *I want to expand globally*, or *I want to run it on my own until I can't anymore.* There are no wrong answers here. Then, on the line below this statement, I want you to write the word *why*."

Ramona paused as her guests dutifully scribbled in their notebooks.

"Now, turn to the third page. I want you to write: *How much money is enough to live the life I want?* Below it? You guessed it. Write the word *why*."

The women did as they were asked.

Ramona was in the zone. "Now, I want you to sit and think. Start by breathing for two minutes. Then, under each question in your notebook, I want you to write the answer. Underneath *each* answer, write the word *why* again. Underneath *those* answers, write *why* again, until the answer behind your *why* is so obvious, it cannot be ignored."

Renee raised her hand. "Ramona, I am not a math person. How do I know how much money I actually need?"

"Renee, when you do the exercise, you'll see it's about money, but it's also not about money at all. It's about what you want your life to look like, and how much money it takes to get that life. Use round numbers, and if you don't have a financial advisor with a plan like Wendy does, just make some assumptions. So many of us are not financially minded, we shy away from numbers. But in this space, we will not shy away, and we will be okay to make mistakes. We will revisit these in more detail when we are ready to enact a plan." Ramona knew she was going to get this question, and she also knew she was going to get resistance around this part of her work. So many women she met hated discussing the fact that they actually want and need money.

The women started writing. The Whisper Way retreat was officially in session now, and Ramona hoped they'd come out of it with some incredible work.

WENDY

Why did I start this business?
I started because I had finally gotten paid on the first business I started, that was draining me, and I was ready to do something I was passionate about.

Why?
Because I felt like in my last business, I was doing it just for the money. And I had something I really believed in, and I wanted to do something that energized me.

Why?
Because what doesn't energize me bores me. Because when I feel stuck or tied to something, I feel really trapped.

Why?
Because above all else, I guess what I really want is freedom. Freedom to do what I love, with people I love, in an industry I love. Financial Freedom. And I will settle for nothing less.

Why?
Because I never felt free as a kid. Because when I was married I didn't feel free. Because I never want to have to depend on anyone. Because being self-made is part of my identity.

I want to ... (What do I want to do with this business?)
I am going to grow this business on my own and get it as far as I can within the next 12–24 months. If I run out of cash, I'll do something else, but if I can maintain my profitability to a point where I'm making what I need, and the margins look healthy and attractive, I'm going to sell this bootstrapped business for 8 million dollars.

Why?
1—Because I'm already profitable when most businesses at my stage aren't
2—Because it's a unique idea, and it's getting traction
3—Because I want to work because I want to and not because I have to, and I don't want to sacrifice my lifestyle
4—BECAUSE I CAN

How much money is enough to live the life I want?
300K per year until I'm 70, so:

EIGHT MILLION DOLLARS!

Why?
Because that is the amount needed to work only because I want to and not because I have to, allowing me to be free.

Exercise

FINDING YOUR
WHY

Let's pause from our story so you can start to define your own *why*! Like Wendy, lots of times women are constantly questioning themselves. Do they want to go big? Do they want to go home? Lean in? Take a nap? As Ramona said in this chapter, it's important to be clear about what you want your life to look like. You may have read or heard of the bestseller *The Seven Habits of Highly Effective People* by Dr. Stephen R. Covey. The second of the seven habits, "Begin with the end in mind," is the spirit behind this thought exercise. And while you may not know exactly what you want your end game to be, if you work your way through these questions, you should come up with a stronger idea of why you're doing what you're doing.

There are lots of theories as to why women vacillate on what they want and are often out of touch with why they want it. Here are three of my favorites:

PERFECTION PARALYSIS

When my friend Reshma Saujani gave her TED talk in Vancouver back in 2016, she addressed the concept of bravery versus perfection.

Most girls are taught to avoid risk and failure. We're taught to smile pretty, play it safe, get all A's. Boys, on the other hand, are taught to play rough, swing high, crawl to the top of the monkey bars and then just jump off headfirst. And by the time they're adults, whether they're negotiating a raise or even asking someone out on a date, they're habituated to take risk after risk. They're rewarded for it. It's often said in Silicon Valley, no one even takes you seriously unless you've had two failed startups. In other words, **we're raising our girls to be perfect, and we're raising our boys to be brave**. (emphasis mine)

What if the reason we want something isn't "perfect" or considered acceptable for a woman to feel? What if what we want doesn't jibe with those around us? Perhaps we don't always know our *why* because we don't think our *why* would be likeable, socially acceptable, or (gasp!) it's imperfect!

THE CONFIDENCE GAP

One of my favorite books is *The Confidence Code* by Claire Shipman and Katty Kay. It talks about the confidence of women and men, and references an internal report from Hewlett Packard, which has been quoted and discussed in many books and articles beyond Shipman and Kay's. This report found that men will apply for a job if they fulfill just 60 percent of the stated qualifications. But women won't apply unless they fulfill 100 percent of them. (Is there a woman alive who is surprised to read this?) But I think it's more than just having us "buck up" and get more confident like the boys. I think for women business owners, it's about losing the fear to dream.

THE MENTAL LOAD

Another theory I have is about distraction, which comes primarily from two sources.

First, there is the invisible mental load that women, and particularly mothers, carry. Sometimes called "emotional labor" or "worry work," the mental load is the labor that goes into leading a family and managing a household—work that is usually invisible to others and typically falls on women to do. A study done by Bright Horizons, a national childcare chain, reinforces this observation: In their report, nearly three-quarters of working moms felt like it was their responsibility to manage their children's schedules, and more than half were on the verge of burnout because of that pressure.

In other words, how can we think about our *why*, when we are thinking about how we need to change the toilet paper roll, order more hand soap, and schedule our gynecologist appointments?

If that all feels overwhelming, it is. And it's no wonder we turn to social media for some good mind-numbing entertainment. That's the second source of distraction! According to a study by Statista, adult women are spending just over an hour a day a day on social media, which serves as an addictive distraction from lots of things, especially deeper thoughts like connecting with what they want and why they want it.

Whatever the reasons may be, many women are disconnected from their *why*. This exercise is designed to help you find it.

THE WHY BEHIND THE WHY

For this exercise, you can use a journal, or simply open a Word doc, but I personally like to use giant wall Post-its. You will need three large pages for whatever you use. Remember, as you're writing, your answers are not public. They don't need to be representative of a "nice" girl or a "good" girl. They only need to feel true.

1. On the top of the first page, write: WHY DID I START THIS BUSINESS?
2. Write whatever answer comes to mind.
3. Underneath the answer, write WHY. Answer why you gave the answer you gave.
4. Continue asking why until you feel you've gotten to the root of the reason. You'll notice that your last answer may have nothing to do with your business at all. That's okay, and important.
5. On the top of the second page, write: I WANT TO. . . .
6. Beneath it, write what you want to do with this business. Do you want to grow it? Sell it? Raise capital? Acquire other businesses?
7. After you write the answer, write WHY. Again, answer why you gave the answer you gave.
8. Continue asking why until you're done asking.
9. On the third page, write: HOW MUCH MONEY IS ENOUGH TO LIVE THE LIFE I WANT?
10. Do your calculations.

The last step is where most of my clients get stuck. I often hear, "Can I just write 'F-U money'?" (For those of you who don't know, F-U money means enough money to never have to work again, and to be able to live the life you want, as extravagantly as possible.) My answer is always, "Sure, if you know what that exact number is!"

How does one find that number? Well, there are a few ways. You should know what you want to make a year based on what you currently make and how comfortable (or not comfortable) you are now. I take a real bottom-up approach to this, which is different than others who work in my space. Most people tend to look at revenue first and then figure out the profit goal—but we're going to begin elsewhere.

First, start with your net worth. Add up everything you've got in the bank, your equity in your home if you own one, your assets. Then, subtract everything you owe to anyone in the world—any outstanding debt, including the balance on your mortgage, student loans, and so on. Now, for non–business owners, this is kind of easy, right? Because 80 percent of their worth is not tied up in a business which may or may not have value at exit. For most entrepreneurs, that's exactly what their net income looks like. It's easy to say, "Oh, my business is worth $8 million, so my net worth is $8.5 million if you think about what I have personally invested plus the business." The problem is, you have *zero* idea if your business is worth that.

So for this exercise, even if it's scary, I want you to remove the business from your net worth. Both its "value" and any debts that are in the name of the business. Pretend the business doesn't exist. Yes, I know, your number just got a lot smaller.

Now, think about how much you need to make each year to live comfortably.

The rule of thumb is: If you want to get to a place where you can comfortably stop working, the amount you need to live each year should equal 4 percent of your total target net worth. Let me explain:

Let's say you need to make $200,000 a year to live comfortably for the rest of your life.

That would mean your net worth would need to be $5 million.

Here's what this means. Whatever the gap is between your current net worth *not* including your business, and the number you just calculated, is the minimum number you need to generate to be comfortable post-exit if this is your last job. If it's only your first act, that's great, but just know you need a plan to ensure you're earning what you need. As you probably know all too well as an entrepreneur, no one is happy or focused when they're worrying about money.

Generally, after I have someone do this exercise, I have them consult with a certified financial planner (CFP). I almost always recommend services from Ellevest, as they are tailored toward women.

Once you understand your *why*, you're ready to move on to a plan that can bring it to life. We'll get there in later steps of the Whisper Way.

REAL-LIFE

WHY

GWEN WHITING

Exit was always at the top of mind for Gwen Whiting when she launched eco-luxe fabric care brand The Laundress back in 2004. It just wasn't for the reasons you'd think.

Gwen spent fifteen years building The Laundress, growing the company to develop over eighty-five products. She did so without any money or savings to fall back on and without raising a dime of outside funding. With only a $100,000 Small Business Administration loan and $250,000 in credit card debt, the brand grew exponentially and developed a cultlike following. Together with her partner, Gwen sold the company to Unilever for a reported $100 million in 2019.

Gwen thought about exit from day 1, but her *why* wasn't about the money at all.

In a personal interview, Gwen told me, "I believed I could only take the business so far on my own. I was determined to solve the problem that I saw—the need for an eco-friendly solution for fabric care and 'dry clean alternatives' for people who care about their clothes and home and deserve better solutions. I wanted this brand to reach as many of those people as possible, and I thought that in order to have that type of impact, a big conglomerate would have to take over to maximize the brand potential."

Gwen's mission-driven desire for impact drove her to relentlessly grow the company while bootstrapping. She described it as spending fifteen years in "never-ending startup mode." She had received interest throughout the years of growth, but in 2019 when Unilever approached her, she knew that it was time to sell.

Although the offer was for life-changing money, it wasn't the money that drew her to a deal with Unilever.

It was the alignment with her *why*—the potential impact a sale like this would have.

With over 128,000 employees across the world, Unilever holds over 400 brand names in over 190 countries. They are a global company with a global purpose. And they were exactly the type of organization that could allow The Laundress to achieve Gwen's desired impact on the world of toxin-free cleaning products. This was her chance to leave a legacy. Furthermore, Unilever had previously acquired Seventh Generation, a household product company whose mission is to transform the world into a healthy, sustainable, and equitable place for the next seven generations. Gwen felt as though she was in good company.

With an exit that was fully aligned with both the company's monetary worth and her *why*, it felt like the timing was right. But that feeling didn't last for long after the sale was completed.

"Unilever did not have any form of onboarding or integration process for the acquisition. They were keen to dismantle existing leadership and systems without thoughtful or qualified replacements. They broke the system and crushed the profitable asset they wanted and acquired. Changes with no process resulted in a full product recall in 2022 that halted all sales and distribution of the brand for nine months."

The reputation of the brand was severely tarnished. And for Gwen, it felt like her entire *why* was shattered in an instant, letting down her trusted suppliers, global business partners, her team/employees, and most importantly her devoted cleaning enthusiasts.

"I always thought I would sell because a bigger company could be able to do more than I could do on my own in advancing my mission. Turns out, they couldn't. My belief was wrong, and this [is] one of my greatest mistakes and greatest lessons learned."

So what do you do when your *why* has been ruined? You act on what you believe in and you get back in the game. "I spent twenty years of my life devoted to the cleaning community I built creating and sharing solutions for clean living, and I felt like I let my customers down [when I sold]," she said.

Gwen had no plans to step back into the laundry room—she was so disenchanted she even went to the dry cleaners! However, with friends, family, and cleaning enthusiasts left "stained and saddened," she felt forced to reclaim her *why* and make a clean start focused on impact—but this time, add in wellness to the equation.

"I suffered during The Laundress years from anxiety, sciatica . . . you name it," she said. "When I thought about my next chapter, I knew that wellness needed to be a major component." To do so, she replaced her signature fine fragrances with strategically blended aromatherapy essential oils, bringing healing energy into cleaning products.

In 2024, five years after her exit and the expiration of her non-compete, Gwen launched The Fill, a private members cleaning community and collection of sustainable products and solutions placing wellness at the heart center of cleaning.

This time, she's not thinking about exit, because for Gwen, she now knows she has different goals and ideas of what success looks like for herself. "I'm still proud to have created the ultimate laundry experience and encouraged people to care about sustainable solutions and treating the environment, themselves, and their belongings with respect and care," said Gwen. "My goal this time around is to create a small, sustainable business that once again offers my loyal community what they've always trusted and counted on me for—products with maximum efficacy and luxury. I'm not ashamed to say, I'm also doing this for me. It's time to reclaim my legacy."

Whether Gwen is selling a company for a reported nine figures or building one that is small and manageable, her *why* is crystal clear and helps guide her in her decision-making.

Chapter Five

Hone In on How

After the exercise was completed, there was a short break, and soon the ladies were refreshed and ready to continue. However, instead of having the women return to their seated circle, Ramona invited them into the dining room, where a long barnwood table took up the majority of the space.

"Oh! Bring your laptops, please!"

Ah, music to Elena's ears. Maybe she could get some work done during this thing, after all.

The women collectively headed back to the foyer area to grab their computers and then filed in to start the next session.

"Hannah, please sit at the head of the table, right there." Ramona gestured to the front of the room.

Hannah approached the front. She had enjoyed the first part of the day, but she had questions.

"Ramona, I feel like my *why* is so clear! I know what I want. I want to change people's lives and help them live longer. I want to improve their collective communities, and I don't want them to pay an arm and a leg to do it. I am clear. I am even clear on the number I want—I moved beyond just paying back my family. I want to build my entire family a better life, and I even think I know how much I'll need to do that." She clasped her hands together as if in prayer. "Thank you for getting me to that point. Can I ask why me, now? Did I seem like I didn't get what was needed out of the exercise?"

"Thanks for that question, Hannah. And you are clearly very mission-driven, and you clearly have a very honest answer about why you want what you want. What we need to talk about is how to get there. Can you open your laptop for me?"

Hannah suddenly became very nervous. Mentally, she prepared to hear the same questions she had heard from the finance bro she'd talked to from her SoulCycle class. He'd asked her about the "lifetime value" of her app user, her CAC—which she later learned was Customer Acquisition Cost. He'd asked about her "churn." Bruh, she had literally launched the app three weeks earlier, and it crashed because her entire community downloaded it at the same time, then bitched about the fact that she was charging. She hadn't known the answer to these questions then, and she only half-knew them now. She just knew how to help people feel great, and it mattered more to her that she could help someone in an underserved community feel great than someone who was paying fifty bucks a class to hear her say "Just ride." She wondered if the women in the room who came from more sophisticated backgrounds already knew what she felt so uneducated about.

"But Ram—"

"Hannah, trust me, okay? Open your laptop."

Hannah opened her laptop.

"I'm going to have you google some terms. Typical valuations for a SaaS company. SaaS means Software as a Service. That is what you are building with your app, right? You're building a subscription program, where users watch licensed videos of you and follow your workouts. Is that correct?"

"Yes." She typed into the search bar "Valuations for SaaS companies" and hit enter. The number of hits was overwhelming.

"As part of The Whisper Group's promise to *keep it real*, I am never going to give you an inflated number that you'll see in the fairy-tale stories in the press. I am going to give you the averages. But it's always good, as a founder, to do your own research. When I did this for my agency, everyone told me I'd get between four and eight times EBITDA, which essentially is a formula that calculates my earnings before interest, taxes, depreciation, and amortization. Don't worry, your accounting software will tell you what this is. For now, just think about it as a multiple of what you make as profit from the business.

"In other words, if I had a million dollars in sales, and it cost me $500,000 to fulfill the orders, and then I spent $250,000 in marketing, rent, and all the stuff needed to operate the business, my business would have $250,000 in profit. That is 25 percent. If my business was worth four to eight times my profits, I would be worth between one and two million dollars. That's on *top* of the 250K I extracted from the business each year in profit as the owner. Does that make sense?"

"I guess," said Hannah, still nervous about the term EBITDA. But Ramona's calculation seemed simple enough.

"The safe valuation I tend to use for SaaS companies like yours as a start is two and a half times revenue or ten times EBITDA. As you grow bigger, you would be worth more, but that's a typical valuation range for a SaaS with revenue in the one to five million dollars a year range. Now, if you exploded and grew, so would your multiple. SaaS companies that are larger are often valued at double or triple that multiple, because companies that make more are typically worth more. With me?"

"I am." Hannah started scribbling in her notebook. "So if I made 100K this year teaching classes outside of SoulCycle, and it's all profit that comes to me, am I worth a million dollars right now?"

"Afraid not," said Ramona. "Just because a valuation says it's possible, it doesn't make it so. Buyers want to buy something they can *scale*. The reason a SaaS is worth so much more than an agency, for instance, is that they're buying more than just the leader and the talent. They're buying the tech and the opportunity to acquire revenue that repeats each month. If you had an app that enough users paid for, you might make 100K a month in revenue pretty easily."

"Easily?" laughed Hannah. "I can't get the app to stop crashing, and folks are chirping when they have to pay ten bucks a month!"

"We'll get to that!" said Ramona, rubbing her hands together gleefully. "Actually, let's keep it really simple and use a revenue multiple here. You said you think they'll pay ten dollars a month?"

"If the app actually works, probably," Hannah said. "And that's low enough that I feel like I'm not taking advantage of anyone and still achieving my mission."

"All right, that's ten thousand users. You'll have to account for a lot here . . ."

Hannah braced herself for all the "CAC, LTV, churn" nonsense that made her head spin.

"But for now, please let's keep things simple. I am of the belief that business owners, especially the women I meet, didn't get into this to become MBAs. So let's not speak like MBAs, okay?"

Hannah exhaled.

"Let's say, between adding new users, and losing some users, you average about 10,000 paying people that use the app each month.

That's $100,000 in revenue a month, or $1.2 million a year. Let's use the revenue multiple we talked about earlier, of two and a half times revenue. Take your annual revenue, and multiply it by 2.5. As a starting point, you'd be worth . . ."

Here came Casey again: *"Three million dollars!"*

"Right," said Ramona. "You'd also want to understand how much profit you'd need to validate that. If the valuations are around ten times EBITDA, you should be making about 300K off of the 1.2 million in sales, which is roughly a 25 percent margin. Because 300,000 times 10 is . . ."

"Three million dollars!" shouted Renee. She looked at Casey, smiling. "Beat ya to it, kid."

"So, for you, Hannah, this is what you need to remember," said Ramona, ticking things off on her fingers as she went. "One: For every dollar you earn through the app, you should theoretically be worth that number times *two and a half.* Two: To make sure you are worth at least that, your profit margin would need to be 25 percent. So, for every dollar you spend, you need to make $1.25."

Hannah was digesting this. It felt scary, but also, somehow, attainable?

"If I made that kind of profit, I could help so many people. And then the sale? It's the icing on the cake."

"Exactly!" Ramona smiled. "Now, I'm going to give you the hard news, and the exciting news. First, this won't be easy. Only 9 percent of small businesses ever end up generating over 1 million dollars a year in revenue. And, as we all know in this room, the deck is stacked against us—but truly, Hannah, the deck is stacked way harder against you. Forget about building seven-figure businesses, only 2.2 percent of small business owners are African American, regardless of business size. But you *are* going to do it.

"I've seen a lot of businesses through the years, Hannah. Here's what I see in you. I see a woman who is on a mission. I see a woman with a following. I see a woman who has built a technology by scraping together peanuts from family and friends. I see a woman who is willing to make the sacrifices to live frugally until she gets what she needs. I see a woman with a unique offering. I see a woman with potential—a woman who can get to that number and more, and I hope you do."

"I do, too," said Hannah, and she meant it. "I just don't know how to do it."

"Ah," said Ramona. "You figured out why you're next."

Ramona asked all of them to open their Whisper Way notebooks.

"One thing that really benefited me throughout my scaling of my first business was the power of a strong peer group. I would like you all now to pretend that you are on the Board of Advisors for OurHour, Hannah's fitness company. You already know why her business exists, and you know why she wants to do what she wants to do: the 'why behind the why,' if you will.

"And you know that, in order to do that, we need to hit a revenue and a profit number that will lead us to a valuation that allows Hannah to achieve her *why*. We know that's *how* she'll be able to accomplish her *why*. But just as we had to get to the 'why behind the why,' we need to learn how to get to the *how*."

"But we have that!" Phoebe interjected. "She needs ten thousand community members to download and pay for her app at ten dollars a month! She can do that! People love Hannah. I've seen her workouts on Instagram, and they're great. She just needs to get out there!"

"How, though?" said Hannah quietly. "I built the app and it crashed, it took me almost two weeks and so much money to fix it. I feel like I missed my shot."

Ramona stepped in. "Before we start the exercise, I want to give your Board of Directors time to ask clarifying questions about the business. These questions should just be factual in nature, don't lead—we are just seeking information here." She banged her fist on the table to give a little knock. "The Board of Directors for OurHour will now come to order! We will be going around the room and each asking questions. Sophia, let's start with you. Ask your question, and select the next person to go, so that they're prepared and we proceed quickly."

"I guess I'll start with this: I know you were delayed with the start because of technical difficulties. How many members have you captured initially that pay for the app? And Wendy, you can go next."

Hannah knew her membership numbers without even having to look. "Well, after I had that issue, I gave away a few free memberships. But most of the memberships are paying members. I have 493 members right now, 482 of which are paid."

"That's a great start!" said Wendy. She knew what it was like to build technology, and how hard it was. She also knew the importance of understanding how your users were engaging with it. "Are the people who pay for the app using it? And have they given you any feedback? Phoebe, you'll go after me."

"In looking at the data, it looks like users are using the app between four and six times a week for fifty minutes at a time. Some power users use it twice a day! I have gotten feedback that the workouts are great. I do occasionally get complaints about price, which I truly can't believe since people shell out so much money for Peloton and SoulCycle." That always bothered Hannah, because she knew her workouts were just as good!

"Give me your total number of followers across all social platforms." Phoebe was in her wheelhouse. She understood the power of influence, and she understood the "it" factor, and she saw it in Hannah. "Okay, and Renee, you're after me."

"This is interesting because I really haven't made a concerted effort to grow my online presence. I've focused on these large community bootcamps. But because I put my Instagram handle up on the signage behind me, it's grown. And of course, the SoulCycle ladies and gents are all up in my business on these channels. So I'd say right now, I have about eight thousand followers on Instagram, and about ten thousand subscribers on YouTube, which is where I've posted my workouts and they've grown organically. Haven't dabbled in TikTok much, and if you look at my Facebook, you'll basically just see the entire Renaissance Arts Academy high school class of 2011."

"Wow," said Renee. "Coffee+ had about 193 fabulous followers until Casey took it over a couple of weeks ago! What are we up to now, honey?"

"We just hit 486!" said Casey excitedly.

"That's great, Casey. And you can go right after me. My question is, Hannah, how big are these community events you host, and how many have you hosted?"

"They're actually really big," said Hannah. "One of the benefits of hosting them in a park is that there is so much space. I even bought a portable stage so everyone could see me. My last class I had two hundred people. People pay what they can; it usually averages out to about fifteen dollars a person between folks who don't pay and some who give a lot because they know what I'm trying to do. I do them about once a month in my neighborhood, and I get some local press coverage too. It's very nice and very meaningful."

"Ever thought about expanding? Perhaps a little Tour De Hannah?" said Casey in her best faux French accent.

"I did do one in the park in West Hollywood by the SoulCycle. That was big and high energy, and I made more, but it didn't feel the same to me. Haven't done any anywhere else."

Casey's head was filled to the brim with ideas. "Your turn, Elena!"

"Who else works on this business with you?"

"My sister is a whiz with numbers. She likes business and has offered to help quite a bit. I'm just afraid if I loop her in, she'll see the numbers for the app and think they're too low. She invested in the business, and I just want my whole family to feel confident that I'll get them a return. I used an offshore company to build the app because it was less expensive, and basically I've done this entirely on my own otherwise."

Boy, did Elena understand that feeling of the weight of the business, and what feels like the world, resting on her shoulders.

"I guess I'm last up," said Ivy. "As a formal board member, let me congratulate you on your fantastic start! And let me ask the final question to you now. What is the road map for content on the site? Is it just your one OurHour workout? Or do you think you'll do more?"

"Oh, I'm glad you asked that one," Hannah said proudly. "The idea of OurHour is that it is an hour that is just for us. We can do what we want with that hour. It started with the traditional OurHour workout—I record about five a week to keep the content fresh. But soon, I want to open this up to other trainers who use their own hour in their own way. OurHour should be more than just Hannah's hour. It should be how my collective community spends their time working on themselves. I see meditation, workshopping, tons of opportunities there. I'm excited to work on the road map because I truly think I'm more of an inspired trainer than a shrewd businesswoman."

Ramona clapped her hands together swiftly. "Let's give a round of applause for the Board of OurHour, and its brave, bold, fantastic CEO, Hannah!"

Next to Ramona was an easel. While the ladies were deep in conversation, Ramona had been busy setting up. Post-it notes had been placed on the table.

"I know you've all been taking notes in your notepads. What I'd like you to do is take your single most actionable suggestion for Hannah—and remember, *how* she is going to achieve her *why* is to get approximately ten thousand paying members. And yes, I know we made this up, but let's use it as a good round number and challenge. What could Hannah do to get started on the right path? No wrong answers here, just thoughts from a group of smart women who understand what it's like to be in her shoes."

One by one they grabbed a Post-it and began writing. It didn't take long at all for them to be lined up, colorful papers in hand, ready to help Hannah solve her "how."

Give Influencers free memberships in exchange for promoting the app.—P

Charge less for an annual subscription instead of monthly to avoid people canceling and protect your numbers.—E

Expand instructors—select ones with influence. Offer them a % of fee for every member they sign up! Like an affiliate . . .—W

Secure the right development team, even if more expensive, to work on the app. Host more in-person events to fund it!—S

Edit all of your YouTube content so that it promotes the app! All social channels should promote the app.—I

Tour De Hannah!

Do a tour but in underserved communities across the country and encourage sign-ups!—C

Become partners with your sister—have her do the business operations while you grow your social media through classes and sharing your magic!—R

Phoebe was the creator of the first Post-it on the board, and as she posted it and turned around, she walked past Hannah and gave her a high five. "You got this, friend."

One by one, the ladies did the same. And after the seventh high five, Hannah was in shock, and in tears. So many of these ideas were ones she had never thought of, and some she'd thought of, but they never felt possible. Suddenly, it all felt achievable. Daunting, sure, but achievable.

"All right now, everyone take your seats." Ramona called them to order. "Hannah, you may not use all of these ideas. You may pick just one. But the idea is, there are a million ways to get to your goal. You will know what's best for your business. That said, tapping into a peer group to help you explore avenues will help you see things that you might not otherwise while stuck in the day-to-day of your business. Your next step is to think through which of these actionable steps, or maybe any new steps that come from this, are worthy of being priorities for you."

"Can we all do this for each other? This is incredible!" Ivy was so inspired, she couldn't sit still in her seat.

"Well," said Ramona, "this exercise is available for any of you at any time, and I certainly hope you continue these relationships beyond this retreat. But in the meantime, Ivy, I'm glad you spoke up! Because after the break, you're next!"

HONE IN ON YOUR
HOW

In our last exercise, you figured out your why. Now that you've gotten honest about the motives behind what you are trying to do, you need to figure out how to get there.

One of the first things I like for founders to do is get an understanding of their value by learning about their industry multiples. Even if you never plan to sell, it is a good benchmark to set for yourself to ensure you are building a healthy business. In other words, you could have a company that generates two million dollars a year, but if it costs two million dollars a year to run it, guess what that company is worth? Bubkes.

By understanding valuations that are done based on simple metrics like EBITDA, it's going to help you do two things. First, you're going to think about your business as an *asset* that has potential value, even if you never sell it—you will know what it is likely worth. Second, it will encourage you to increase the value of that asset, which will actually have you make more money. If you have an agency that is valued at eight times EBITDA, then every single dollar you put into your pocket in a calendar year is worth eight. So, when you spend a dollar, you're also kind of spending eight! Understanding those multiples helps you think more clearly about what you spend.

For most business owners reading this, your EBITDA multiple will be somewhere in the range of three to seven.

There are lots of ways to find this number. You can talk to an advisor, broker, or investment banker. You can google "(industry you're in) acquisition" and search news. You can visit sites like PitchBook.com, TheyGotAcquired.com, and Acquire.com. But no matter what you find, every industry will never have one finite multiple number. There is always a range.

When I sold my agency, the average multiples were anywhere between four and eight times EBITDA. My EBITDA was around two million dollars. Was I going to walk away with eight? Or was it sixteen? And how would I know? The "how" is about determining how you are going to land on the best-in-class end of that range. When you implement the Whisper Way, you are implementing a process that is dedicated to getting you as much damn money in your hands as possible.

Here's another real nugget of wisdom. There are financial acquirers, and then there are strategic acquirers. Strategic acquirers often look to buy your business in order to expand their products or eliminate competition. Financial buyers, like private equity funds and family offices, look to buy businesses they can grow and sell after a period of time. Often, strategic buyers are willing to pay more for companies than financial buyers, since they are better placed to realize synergistic benefits almost instantly. That's why it's important to think about who might be a strategic acquirer for your business, even if you never intend to sell it.

For this exercise, please research the multiples of your industry. I recommend choosing the one that is on the lower side, just to keep your head in check, and to avoid building a business based on delusions of grandeur. If you get there, great, but I am perpetually rooted in reality, just like Ramona and her Whisper Group.

Next, write down three potential individuals or businesses that would be strategic acquirers for your company. I'll give you an example. When I was running Likeable, I became convinced that Reese Witherspoon's production company, Hello Sunshine, should be our acquirer. I was creating killer social content for women, and they were creating films for women. Because I had an insufficient Roar score (which we'll cover in chapter 10), I never reached out. Soon after, they acquired companies and executed on some mergers to launch a podcast network and a VOD network featuring interviews with women, exactly like the ones I did. I wonder what would have happened if I had proactively networked with them. Because I didn't, I'll never know.

Then, look up the heads of each of those companies on LinkedIn, and see how far removed you are from them, or other senior executives at the company.

Then, get ready to reach out. It's fine to say, "I just want to be on your radar." It's fine to connect without an agenda. It's fine to say, "Hey, I think we'd be a great fit for acquisition." Honestly, you need to do what feels authentic to you, and there are many stories featured on my podcast, *The Exit Whisperer*, that yielded a good result. (Take a listen, I promise you'll extract some great ideas for identifying acquirers!) You miss 100 percent of the shots you don't take. So take the shot.

"HOW" EXERCISE

1. My average industry EBITDA multiple is _____.
2. My EBITDA last year was _____.
3. My EBITDA this year will be _____.
4. Based on that, I'm worth about _____ today. (Then take a look back at your WHY exercise and see what the gap is.)
5. To exit for the number I want, I would need to have _____ EBITDA.
6. The following would be amazing strategic acquirers for my company:

   _____

   _____

   _____

7. I am most closely connected to the following people at those companies:

   _____

   _____

   _____

8. In the next 12 months, I promise myself I will:

   _____

   _____

   _____

It's great to envision your exit, and to set an EBITDA target based on that dream. It's another thing to know the steps to take to actually get there. In our fable, Hannah has a mock Board of Directors comprised of her peers that asks her a ton of questions and then brainstorms some potential options with her.

In my book *Work It: Secrets for Success from the Boldest Women in Business*, I talk about forming a FAB PAB, short for a "Fabulous Personal Advisory Board," to help advise you on all aspects of your life. For this, you need something a little bit different.

Having peers who understand what you are trying to do in business is key. That's why I am such an avid proponent of networks. Whether Entrepreneurs' Organization, Young Presidents' Organization, Women Presidents Organization, Chief, or the Female Founder Collective, it seems that every day, there are new groups popping up. Entrepreneurship in itself is a unique struggle, and when you surround yourself with other business owners, you have an opportunity to feel seen and be vulnerable in a way you might not with others who haven't lived it.

At Likeable, I had an advisory board that consisted of chief marketing officers, lawyers, accountants, and business strategists. They were great. But when I really wanted to dig myself out of a hole, I had a group of entrepreneurs on speed dial.

Here's why it's good to speak with other entrepreneurs:

1. You can feel *safe*. I remember one of my friends who ran a business looked at me and said, "Carrie, I made thirteen thousand dollars this year." This was shocking because to the outside world, she looked like a tremendous success. And in many ways, she was; she was just building toward something that either would or wouldn't pan out in a big way. Someone who isn't in this daily struggle could never really understand that.

2. They are *scrappy*. When my back was up against a wall, I always called a fellow entrepreneur to help me talk it through. There is no one more enterprising than a person who has

risked it all, and they understand when you need to solve a problem that feels unsolvable.

3. They have *connections*. Generally, if you've built something from nothing, you've not done it entirely on your own. I remember an entrepreneur who once introduced us to a banker he knew who would issue us a line of credit when we were almost out of cash and no one would take a chance on us. Entrepreneurs have stood where you stood, and they are prepared to help you over the hump.

For me personally, I tend to surround myself with female, and specifically minority, entrepreneurs, mostly because that's who I advise. But also, they understand some of the intricacies of lack of access to funding, sexism, and sitting as the only woman in rooms full of men. That's not a prerequisite, but I will tell you that has helped me more times than I can count.

For this exercise, I'd like you to draw a table like the table in Ramona's dining room. Imagine the table seats six to eight people, and the people you'll invite are all entrepreneurs. (Ideally you know these entrepreneurs, but if not, remember, they're only a connection away. Try to avoid people who are completely unattainable to you.)

Imagine you're seated at the head. Who is sitting with you? Write the names next to each of the chairs.

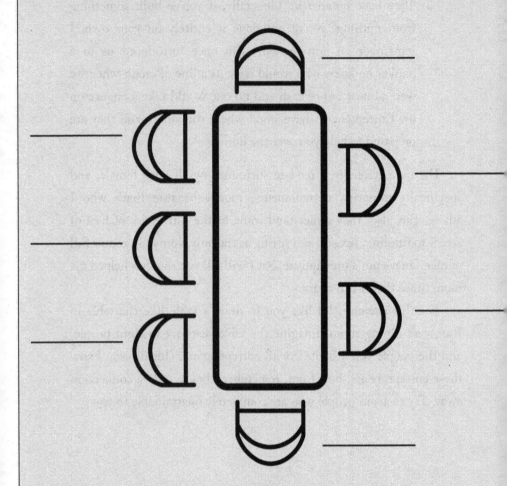

If you're struggling to come up with who would be sitting with you, it's time to join a network. Check out the ones I listed above for some inspiration.

REAL-LIFE
HOW

KASS LAZEROW

Kass Lazerow had already started and sold a business with her husband when they launched Buddy Media in 2007, previously selling GOLF.com during the dot-com era. However, that exit was small in comparison to what she and her husband, Mike, were able to accomplish with Buddy Media. Just five years after starting Buddy Media, the leading social media marketing platform, Kass and Mike sold the business to Salesforce for a deal with a reported value of over $745 million.

The market generally has a multiple range that acquisitions in a particular industry fall between. That multiple is based either on profit, or, in some cases, on revenue. If you've built a strong business, the idea is that you can be valued at the top of that multiple, or even past it, to sell for the most money possible. However, if you calculated the "multiple" on an acquisition like this, it would be astronomical. This deal was considered a strategic acquisition—meaning that the price was based on just how badly the acquirer wanted and needed the company. If there is a strategic reason an acquirer wants you, and they see how acquiring your company can change their business for the better, then the sky is the limit on the valuation. But how did Kass and Mike manage to secure a valuation of this size, and so quickly after starting?

Mike was certainly a visionary, hitting the timing of the social media wave perfectly. And he was able to secure initial investments from investors who had previously invested in their first startup. But if you ask me, the real way that they were able to command this kind of value was based on some key decisions from Kass as an operational leader.

Two of them? Investing early and often in marketing, PR, and in legal.

"We had a great team for marketing and PR. PR and a general counsel was one of my first two hires," said Kass on my podcast, *The Exit Whisperer*. "I hired those departments [first], which is unheard of, but I think that allowed us to kind of catapult other companies."

The duo decided that if they were to make a splash, they had to target large brands—specifically the *Fortune* 500. To do so, they needed contracts that worked for those brands and that also provided them with the necessary protections.

Kass felt strongly that part of the reason she was able to get *Fortune* 500 contracts approved was that she "had all our contracts in line" due to having hired an in-house general counsel so early on in the company.

Once she had these premier brands contracted, it was time to let the world know exactly the type of company Kass and Mike were building. "For marketing, I believe that perception is reality."

Kass and her team came up with an idea that was novel for a company focused on powering digital advertising. She pitched the board to fund a traditional print media campaign, one that would run as billboards in airports. The copy was simple: "Eight out of the top ten Fortune 500 companies partner with Buddy Media to power their connections."

The campaign cost a million dollars, which was a significant amount of their funding at the time. But Kass was adamant that it was necessary.

"The board was shocked. I wanted a million dollars and they said, 'Wait, you're going to spend a million dollars from November 15th to January 15th? You've got to be kidding!' And I fought. It was not an easy battle. . . I finally got it through and, crazy enough, it worked."

Not only did every customer know that Buddy Media was growing and servicing the world's biggest brands. But also, their potential acquirers knew too. And that made the company pretty darn irresistible.

For Kass's *how*, the secret was in how she thought about winning. "My dad taught me basketball, he was a basketball player in college, and it was time to box out the competition."

It was their impressive client roster that helped bring Salesforce to the table. When Salesforce CEO Marc Benioff discussed the deal, he often quoted the following stat from a 2012 Gartner report: "By 2017, CMOs will spend more on tech than CIOs, and 15 percent of that spending will be on CRM, or customer-relationship management—Salesforce.com's bread-and-butter." Mark was looking to get in with CMOs of *Fortune* 500 companies. And all he had to do was look up from his phone while walking through the airport to see exactly which company had contracts with those CMOs.

Buddy Media sold to Salesforce in the fall of 2012, for an estimated astounding 8x revenue multiple. In comparison, their competitor Vitrue sold to Oracle in that same year for a 3x multiple. They offered similar services. One of the main differences, however, was that Buddy Media had a *how* that was planned and executed methodically by Kass.

Chapter Six
Improve Your Income

"**B**reak" included a fabulous catered farm-to-table dinner under a gazebo on Ramona's sprawling remote property. The women laughed together, drank wine, and shared war stories of life deep in the trenches of entrepreneurship. As servers cleared their plates, Ramona (who had changed into a red floral gown for dinner that appeared to match her Pinterest-inspired table) informed them that the after-dinner session would begin and was the last of the day.

"Ramona, I'm so tired!" said Ivy. "My brain doesn't work post-dinnertime!"

"Actually," said Ramona, "that's exactly what I want from you, Ivy. No details. No solutions. My sense is that your brain has been in overdrive this entire time—I can just about see the wheels turning. And as a former agency owner, I know that's pretty darn normal. But one thing you said earlier really struck me. You talked a lot about being weird with money and a fear of being homeless. I only want to ask you . . . when did that shift happen in your mindset? Can you target the moment that you started worrying like this?"

Ivy took a sip of her wine and thought about it. Her defenses were down. "I guess when I ran agencies before I owned my own, I always felt superior. Like I knew that *only* I could do it better. I could win every pitch. I could make us more profitable. I should be in charge. I was also pissed off. I was pissed at the fifty-hour workweeks. I was pissed that we were all worked into the ground. And I suppose that gave me the courage to stop talking about how I would do it better, and actually *do* it better. When my kids were little and I started the business, I felt like I was on top of the world. The queen of balance: I took on a few projects, I was home for the kids, and it was great! But I wanted more. That's when I positioned Major Makers as a hotshot new agency, and when that worked, I think I still was feeling good.

"If I'm being honest, two things happened. As I started adding staff, expenses kept growing. And even though I always had the revenue to offset it, managing the cash was nerve-racking. I think that was the start of it. But what really did it was when I felt the camaraderie of the team. I *loved* that feeling, but suddenly, I started feeling afraid that I would lose business, and then I'd have to let people go. And then we won the huge client, and I felt totally dependent on them. In order to keep my people, I had to overservice the client. In order to overservice the client, I had to do the very thing that made me leave agency life in the first place! We all started working around the clock. And I just hate that for my team."

"But Ivy," said Phoebe, "how the heck do you jump from that to thinking you'll be homeless?"

Ivy wasn't sure.

"Don't answer that too fast," said Ramona. "Sit until the answer comes to you."

"Truly, it doesn't make any sense," said Ivy. "I guess I feel a lot of pressure. I'm the family breadwinner, so there's financial pressure. And then there's the whole ego thing. If I spent the majority of my career thinking that I can do it better, and then I don't, and I fail, well, what does that say about me?"

She felt a lump rising in her throat.

Ramona put her hand over Ivy's, in solidarity. "Sometimes, what's holding us back in business has nothing to do with business at all. But the challenges you have? They are real business challenges. And you have to be in the right space to tackle them."

"I just don't know what's going to happen next," said Ivy, her voice quivering.

"Try saying that again, but with confidence, curiosity, and excitement," said Ramona.

"*I just don't know what's going to happen next!*" yelled Ivy, laughing and crying at the same time.

"Nobody does," said Sophia.

Just then a server came over. "May I offer you all more wine?"

"I'll have the white," Ivy said.

"Want to know how to tackle your challenge, Ivy?" said Ramona. "Try the *red*."

"What?"

"Okay, not literally. But I'm going to teach you—and by the way, this applies to all of you—an easy trick to remember to make sure your business income is damn impressive, instead of paralyzing. And believe it or not, you're going to think of it every time you order red wine, or really any time you think about the color red.

"Usually, when you think about money, red's not such a great color, right? You don't want to be in the red! But that's not what I'm talking about here. Red is a very important color for women, actually."

Ramona held up her hands to show off her cherry-red manicure. "Throughout history, women were banned from wearing red lipstick or red nail polish, so as to not *attract* the male gaze."

"Oh, I saw a TikTok about this!" exclaimed Casey. "A girl encouraged other girls to wear red lipstick and see if more guys liked them because of it!"

"I've seen that too—pretty degrading, if you ask me," said Ramona. "But for many, many years, women have taken that theory and turned it on its head. They took the color that was purported to attract men, and flipped it to claim their power as women. Like, way back in the early 1900s, suffragettes wore red lipstick as a symbolic rebellion and to express support for women's rights. And even in more recent days, I've seen news stories about women activists and protesters in Central and South America wearing red lipstick for unity. So whenever we see red, I hope we remember that we can channel our collective power—and remember how it can be used to make our income impressive, too."

Phoebe whispered to Sophia, who was seated right next to her, "This shit is definitely going in my next spoken word piece!" Sophia nodded, eager to hear where Ramona was going with this—and what it had to do with business. Ramona continued.

"When we are talking about a business's revenue, we need it to be strong. Not all revenue is created equal, you know. Many people run businesses where their revenue is not strong, but they don't realize it since they are making a lot of money in the moment. Usually, they realize it when they are on the brink of collapse, either financially or mentally. When you have what I call 'impressive income'—the *I* in WHISPER—you have a business that will make you more money, will have you working less, and will be attractive to acquirers should you ever choose to sell. Is there anyone here who feels they could make their income more impressive?"

All hands shot up.

"To make your income impressive, order the *R-E-D* and make sure your income is *recurring*, *expected*, and *diversified*. Let's go into each of these. One-off projects or sales are not recurring unless you figure out a way to make them so. Recurring income is when clients or customers renew with you. They order your cookies each month, they sign yearlong contracts for marketing services, they have a membership—that kind of thing. Recurring revenue makes your revenue more predictable. The longer a contract, the better. In fact, I'd rather see you charge less for recurring business than charge more for a large one-time project. Because that recurring business is predictable.

"The business that you have should *be* expected, and *have* clear expectations. And no, those aren't the same thing! When I say business should be expected, I mean I want you to be able to predict or forecast your income with ease. Whether you have a sales team, you run paid ads, or you grow current accounts each year by adding geographic locations or services, you should know that if you invest x, you get y. It doesn't have to be exact, but it should be based on some form of data. And as far as clear expectations, those are especially important for a services business like yours, Ivy. Your projects or retainers must be clearly scoped. You need to state clearly what is in the scope and what is not. My guess is that your large client is guilty of scope creep, and you're going way above and beyond what is within your current agreement out of fear of losing them."

Ivy nodded in agreement. No matter what her statements of work said, she and her team would almost always over-deliver for clients. That especially pertained to her largest client, who was extremely demanding. When it came to that client, Ivy felt like she had no other choice.

"And finally, revenue must be diversified. If you have your entire business based on one client, you are at risk. If you have your product sold in only one mass retailer, you are at risk. And finally, if you have only one offering, it is possible that you are at risk. You want your income to have insurance against loss. I remember when I was first starting out in agency life, a consultant looked me dead in the eye and said, 'Only one thing is certain in this business. Clients will fire you.' The way to grow a business is to reduce 'churn.' Churn is basically business speak for the rate at which you lose clients. You want to protect against losing clients, while adding new ones. But sometimes we focus so much on not losing our single biggest client that we miss out on other opportunities. Times change, clients change, needs change, and your income needs to be protected against those changes."

Maybe it was because she was stuffed to the brim, but this conversation gave Elena a stomachache. She had a college consulting business, and this was going to be rough to figure out. Why would clients return to her once their child got into college? If she was successful, her clients wouldn't need her. But at least this whole thing was interesting. "Ramona, do you have any examples?"

"Sure!" said Ramona. "I had a friend who had an agency business that produced YouTube videos for clients. They would do one at a time at 5K a pop, and clients came in through discovery, because her agency had pretty good SEO. And their clients would often come back, but they didn't know when or how. So they started a package of monthly videos. Instead of 5K a pop, they charged $4,000 a month for twelve months. Clients were able to then reserve the team they wanted because they had them on a retainer.

"Soon, they realized that TikTok was gaining traction. Suddenly, short-form video was very important. They started including bonus TikTok videos in their packages, which caught on. They started a TikTok on-demand product, where a client paid them 1K a month, and when a relevant trend came up, they'd produce a TikTok using the trending audio.

"The one thing they struggled with was how to grow beyond the organic search parameters. So they started to invest in social advertising. They charged $500 for a single TikTok—which was a one-off project, but the idea was to convert the client to the monthly TikTok subscription. They realized that they were averaging one new client for the TikTok package off every $50 they spent. So, at a 10 percent cost of sale, with a potential to convert that sale into a $12,000 recurring customer, they now had expected new business income in addition to their organic incoming leads and their current clients that had been converted to retainer."

"That's so interesting!" said Ivy. "Did they take on single YouTube video projects anymore?"

"Well, they had a very hard time saying no, at first. So what they did was they decided to price them at a premium. They started charging *double* the amount of the retainer clients for single videos. Sometimes, they won them. That was fine. But more often than not, they were saying no to bad revenue. And that takes discipline." Ramona turned and looked at Elena. "By the way, Elena, solopreneurs can refine their offerings to be repeatable, too. This TikTok strategy would have worked for a solo social media consultant as well as for a large agency."

Wendy took a sip of her wine and spoke. She was feeling a little sassy. "Okay, Ramona, that's all well and good. But what about Ivy's case, where she has one big client that pays for almost her entire staff? You're not replicating that with a TikTok ad!"

"You're right about that, Wendy. When you are working with enterprise clients, it takes a lot more time and effort. Same with Sophia. She made getting WholeHeart into Whole Foods seem easy! The story was downright magical, a chance meeting at her children's school. But imagine what it would take to get another major retailer like that. So I want to validate that. But my answer would be that when your entire business is focused on one customer like that, your focus as the leader should be to set a plan that allows you to win one more, and then one more, and so on. *And*, you should consider diversifying enough that you can build around that customer. Whether that's selling product online, or offering lower-priced retainers for a different services product, there's always a way to incorporate some RED into your revenue."

Sophia held her glass in the air. "With that, I'd like to propose a toast. To Ivy, for her vulnerability. To Ramona, for her methodology. To all of us, for taking the time to be here. And to RED!"

"To RED," they said, and clinked their glasses together.

MAKE YOUR INCOME
IMPRESSIVE

Hopefully, you're using these little breaks from our story to work on your own stuff. And what's at the top of most entrepreneurs' minds? Revenue. No matter what business you're in, revenue is the most basic measure of how you're doing as a business. Are you generating income from your efforts? If not, the business is likely not a business at all.

But, as Ramona said in this chapter, all revenue is not created equal. An exercise that I do with women regularly is ask them to rate their revenue. If their revenue is project based, if they personally are needed to execute the project, and if the time taken to win the business costs more than the time needed to execute it, then it's not revenue that is the sign of a healthy growing business. And while an exception *can* be made looking at "solopreneur" businesses, generally, you want to have a business that can make money even when you're personally not working. You'll find some of these revenue questions in the Whisper Score Assessment, but for a quick analysis, ask yourself these four questions:

1. Do customers come to me one time, or do they repeat/renew at regular intervals?
2. Can I accurately forecast my revenue for the next year?

3. Do I sell more than one product or service?
4. Does no one customer represent more than 20 percent of my revenue?

I've listed some ways to tackle each of the areas we address to make your income more impressive using the RED acronym, and I've also provided some high-level descriptions. See if any of them inspire you before you start the exercise.

RECURRING REVENUE

Recurring revenue is typically defined as income a company can predict it will earn from consistent, stable transactions in the future. Most one-time purchases do not qualify as recurring revenue. What makes recurring revenue so attractive? As a business owner, you are able to know what you're going to be earning each month. It's predictable and allows you to project your payroll and your own income with relative ease. As a buyer of a business, recurring revenue is the best kind of revenue to buy, because it is typically contracted, and you can more easily predict cash flow.

Here are some ways to increase your recurring revenue:

Longer-Term Contracts: Many companies sell their offerings via a contract. While a customer may pay month-to-month, they're committed to the length of the contract, whether it's one year or even longer. It may be possible to cancel, but there are usually penalties built in. Although contracts do not typically renew automatically, they tend to include opportunities to extend or revise at the end of the term. Whenever I advise a client, I tell them to go for as long a contract as they can. In order to do that, sometimes my clients provide bonus add-ons for signing a contract of that size (giving the client one month free, as an example), or sometimes they provide a discount if it doesn't devalue the brand.

Subscription Revenue: The difference between contract revenue and subscription revenue is simply that with a subscription, the customer pays in advance for a service or product that is used in a specific period of time. The subscription renews automatically at the end of the payment period unless it is canceled. Examples of subscription revenue that you know of are streaming services like Netflix. Gym memberships are also subscriptions. There are also less-typical subscriptions that are created to improve the income of a company. When I ran a social media agency, I built something called the Content Credit System, where clients subscribed to a certain number of credits each month, and redeemed them for types of content.

Supplementary Purchases: In business school, this is where everyone oohs and aahs at the razor blade model: You sell razors, and customers need to perpetually buy razor blades. Supplementary purchases in the services business can be as simple as upsells. An agency that sells a low retainer for social base services can sell incremental trending content creation. A lawyer can be kept on a base retainer, and then services can be expanded at a time of crisis.

EXPECTED INCOME WITH CLEAR EXPECTATIONS

The renowned investor and philanthropist Warren Buffet said, "Risk comes from not knowing what you're doing."

Understanding your revenue—how to accurately forecast it, and plan your expenses against it—makes your income much less risky.

And you're not the only one who should know what to expect out of your business. Your customers should know what to expect, too. So here, you want to focus on making sure that you will have income that you can expect, and that you can deliver services or products that meet the expectations required of the money that they spent on it. Otherwise, your income is at risk.

Here are some ways to set clear expectations for expected income:

Clear Contracts, Clear Communication: Everything starts with clear communication. If you are clear in your contracts, you can avoid what's called "scope creep," which is clients pushing for services that are outside of your agreed-upon parameters. But even with a clear scope, clients may still push the boundaries of what they can ask for within a contract. The only way to combat that is to be in frequent communication with clients around your contracts. The same goes for being able to predict your revenue. If you are in a business where that prediction is harder to do, communicating with your customers will clue you in on how they're feeling and give you an idea of if they are happy enough with your products or services that they'll renew. Running an online business where you don't speak to your customers? Check your email open rates, time spent on your site, and more to identify the key indicators of renewal or cancellation, and build your messaging around those insights.

I once knew a business owner whose mood was like the weather, except instead of changing when the sun was out, it changed whenever the latest economic report hit the trades. If the Fed raised rates, he was convinced the business would go under, and if the jobs report was good, he was convinced the business would soar. The reality is, had he spent time actually talking to his customers instead of reading the news, he would've had a much clearer picture of his business. There are reports, and then there's reality. Do try and look for macro trends, but pay attention to your customers first and foremost, as they will be the most likely to accelerate or tank your growth.

Understand Your Customer Acquisition Costs: When you understand how much it costs to win a new customer, your revenue becomes much more predictable. How does new business come in today? Do you run ads? Do you have an outbound sales team? Do you have a formal referral program? Whatever it is, try to quantify the amount you invest in it versus the amount it yields. What is the return, and how can you improve upon that? And if you tell me that your growth strategy to this point has been "word of mouth," I'm going to tell you that your income, while likely quite good, can be way more impressive if you figure out a way to operationalize that word of mouth. Examples of that would be an affiliate program or a referral bonus.

When in Doubt, Analyze Historical Data: For those of you who run a business based on your gut instincts, your eyes may have glazed over when I talked about Customer Acquisition Costs! Instead of obsessing about the fact that you don't really get it, just think about it as what you know for sure about your business based on past performance. You wouldn't be where you are today if you weren't able to make smart decisions relatively quickly. Take a look at your past revenue as far back as three years if you have been in business that long. How has it changed? Are your top customers growing? Are they shrinking? Now take a look at your revenue by quarter. Do you have busy seasons? Slower seasons? To make your income more impressive, ask yourself how to keep the large customers growing and keep the revenue trends strong.

DIVERSIFIED INCOME

I've long been a believer in the power of focus. But hyper-focus on any one thing leaves you vulnerable. Whether it's focusing on one customer, or offering only one stock-keeping unit, or offering only one service and being rigid in your offering, too narrow a lens can break a business.

Diversification allows businesses to increase organizational capabilities. It means expanding your operations, adding more products or services, or tapping into other markets, and it's a very valuable tool to protect you from loss of income.

Here are some ways to diversify your income:

New Products: It's so important to expand your offerings to maintain relevance, no matter what business you're in. Even if you have the perfect product that is selling like hotcakes, you do not know what tomorrow will bring. The market is fickle, and you should have a product road map to diversify beyond your current state—forever innovating.

New Customers: No customer should ever represent more than 20 percent of your revenue, but for many business owners, that is simply not the case. The only way to reduce that percentage is to increase your income from other sources, whether they are existing clients with smaller spends, or new customers. Set a plan to win new customers, while making sure your current customers are well serviced, and you have a winning formula.

Expand Your Geographic Footprint: This is pretty self-explanatory, but opening up a new location, especially if you can predictably replicate the success of your current footprint, can be a winning strategy. This works especially well with retail and event-based companies.

Establish Vertical/Niche Expertise: Becoming the absolute expert in a certain niche can help a business grow exponentially. Sometimes this comes in the form of servicing *only* customers in that vertical, but other times, you can build a product or service specifically for a niche market and use that to create scalable predictable revenue. My friend Martha Vetter founded R/P Communications, a PR firm that was a generalist agency, meaning they worked with lots of clients. She found that new business revenue was relatively unpredictable, so she set up a division that worked specifically with hospice organizations. A passion point for Martha, this niche was small but mighty, and best of all, it was easy to win new clients in the vertical because her firm was able to show that they had helped other hospice organizations. This more productized approach eventually grew to represent a decent portion of her business, with revenue that she could accurately predict.

BONUS: Acquire Your Competitors: Here's something that most women don't think about when growing their business. We are hesitant to think about being acquired, but for most of us, the thought of actually being the one acquiring doesn't even cross our minds. In reality, acquiring businesses is not difficult or beyond your scope. There are a variety of SBA and bank loans available to women, and if you have an existing business with assets, acquiring a business can be even easier than you think. There are many sites like Acquire.com, BizBuySell.com, and TheyGotAcquired.com that showcase businesses for sale. When evaluating businesses for sale, you would use the same exact methodology, but for the prospective acquisition instead of for your own firm. Instead of making your own income impressive, you're evaluating how impressive and long-lasting the revenue is of the company you're acquiring. It is my hope that, eventually, there are many more of us sitting on this side of the table.

HAVE THE RED

For this exercise, you'll see that I've filled this RED wine goblet with each of these top-level tactics. These are very general, and designed that way to apply to as many businesses as possible.

RED

Create a compelling reason to sign for longer-term contracts

Create a subscription

Supplementary purchases

How Can I Make My Revenue Recurring?

Clearly written contracts

Strong client relationships

Understand my CAC (Customer Acquisition Cost)

Analyze historical data to predict revenue

How Can I Make My Revenue/Delivery Expected?

New products

Expand geographic footprint

New customers

Acquire competitors

Establish vertical/domain-level expertise

Focus on niche

How Can I Diversify My Revenue?

Now, I'd like you to think about your specific business. In the goblet, answer each of the questions more specifically for you. If you have an executive team, feel free to loop them in on this, or tap into any advisors you have, informal or formal, who may know your business well enough to share an insight.

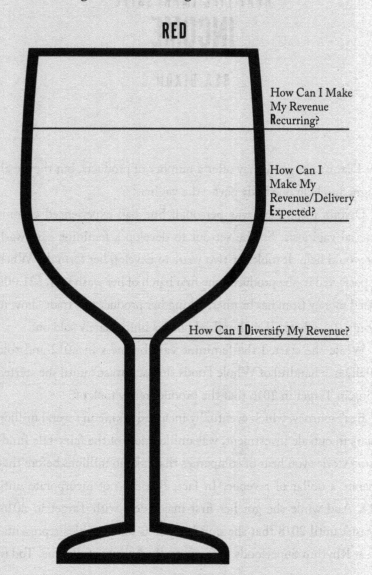

RED

How Can I Make My Revenue Recurring?

How Can I Make My Revenue/Delivery Expected?

How Can I Diversify My Revenue?

REAL-LIFE IMPRESSIVE
INCOME

BEA DIXON

Bea Dixon's company may offer a number of products, but they're all designed to help one body part—the vagina.

Dixon's inspiration was personal: She had experienced chronic bacterial vaginosis. So she set out to develop a feminine care wash that would help. It took her two years to develop her formula. When she perfected it, she produced the first batch of her wash with $21,000 in seed money from her brother, taking her product to a trade show in Georgia . . . where all six hundred bottles immediately sold out.

While she started the feminine care business in 2012 and sold initially in a handful of Whole Foods stores, it wasn't until she started selling in Target in 2016 that the product really took off.

Bea's journey, which eventually included taking in several million dollars in outside investment, was unlike most of the fairy-tale fundraising stories you hear of companies that take in millions before they generate a dollar of revenue. In fact, Bea did not incorporate until 2014. And while she got her first major deal with Target in 2016, it wasn't until 2018 that she quit her job as an area sales representative at Rhythm Superfoods to focus on the business full-time. Today,

The Honey Pot Company products are sold at top retailers including Walmart, Walgreens, and CVS.

Expanding beyond Target as a major retailer was one strategy for growth, but how else could Bea make her income impressive? The global beauty and personal care products market size was estimated at $518 billion in 2022, with $40 billion of that coming from the feminine hygiene market. The competition is ferocious, and once you take in investor money, growth is no longer a desire, but a demand.

As Dixon said on the *Entreprenista* podcast, "Venture capitalists are interested in, 'I'm gonna give you some money right now, and when the fuck am I gonna get my money back, and by the way, that shit needs to 5x, 6x, 10x, plus.'"

So what were the options to ensure that her income would continue to grow at the rate required? One thing that Bea credits to her growth is focusing on the diversification of products. On the *Entreprenista* podcast, she talked about her Product Innovation Pipeline. "You've managed to get your product on a shelf at a retailer, right? Every year you're going to be meeting with that retailer . . . It's called a Category Review season. Every time you go to sit down with that fucking buyer, you better be showing them something new."

On the *SistersInc.* podcast from Black Enterprise, Bea confirmed that she has up to "ten years of innovations written down." That's a truly impressive product road map—a concept I introduced a few pages ago. Yours might not be as long as Bea's, but having concrete plans and ideas for new offerings will help you almost put your product diversification on autopilot.

Bea chose to focus on product innovation because it was her superpower. When the podcast hosts asked how she thinks of the products that she creates, she says, "How does a painter know how to paint. You know what I'm saying? Like, how does a singer know how to sing. The thing is, is I don't paint and I don't sing, but I make skincare products."

The Honey Pot continues to offer new products. As Dixon told a CNN Business reporter, "We have new product launches coming. We're entering new areas like adult incontinence products."

Bea thought long and hard about exiting, and grappled with the decision until 2024, when The Honey Pot sold the majority of the business to Compass Diversified Holdings for a record $380 million.

In that CNN Business article, Dixon was quoted as saying, "Look, exit creates wealth. In Black communities, traditionally if you talk about exiting your business, it's seen as you sold out." But she said it was "part of doing business," viewing it instead as an opportunity to start another company. The selling of The Honey Pot will allow Bea the resources to build new brands, and help other women and her own community build businesses. And if that's not the goal, I don't know what is.

Chapter Seven
Secure Your Secret Sauce

Sophia was up at sunrise. She was used to waking up on her children's schedule, and Jack was a take-no-prisoners kind of kid when it came to waking up before the sun did. She reflected on the evening. It had been years since she'd had a girls' night out like that, let alone one that was so profound.

What would she do this early, with no one else to prepare for their day? She didn't need to pack anyone's lunch, or do anyone's laundry, or track anyone's screen time. She could just be.

She opted to take a morning walk around the property. The plants were all native, and the air felt crisp and clean. She felt herself actively trying to calm her mind. Even with no demands on her time, her thoughts ping-ponged around in her brain, popping from wondering what the kids were doing to wondering if the purchase order from Whole Foods had come through, to thinking about that stupid product she saw on the shelf that looked like a literal carbon copy of Whole-Heart. She couldn't remember if the fridge was properly stocked for

Greg in her absence, and she was fairly certain she'd forgotten to add the birthday party that Vivian had RSVP'd to on the calendar. How does anyone do any of this, and was she really cut out for any of it?

Before she realized it, it was time to get ready and meet everyone to start the day.

When Sophia stepped into the main living area, she saw Ramona's eyes directed toward her, and she could sense that she was next. Ramona gestured for her to take a seat next to her. She wondered which part of the assessment she'd failed the most miserably. *Let's see,* she thought, *it's called the WHISPER program—and we tackled Wendy's "Why," and Hannah's "How," and Ivy's "Income" . . . I guess that means I'm here to work on my . . .*

"Gooooood morning!" Ramona trilled, cheery as could be. "I hope you all got a restful sleep and are feeling confident this morning! Because today, we are going to work on what makes you and your business different from everyone else. I like to call that your 'Secret Sauce.'"

Oh, crap, thought Sophia. *Everything that was special about my business is now sitting right next to my product on the Whole Foods shelf. But maybe that's why I'm here.*

"I guess I'm up then?" said Sophia. Ramona nodded.

Renee gave her hand a squeeze. "This is a tough one, hon. But we've all got this struggle."

Sophia squeezed her hand back. She was ready to try, and that was the most she could ask of herself.

"Tell us about WholeHeart, Sophia. What makes it different?" said Ramona. She was going to approach this topic softly, because if there was one thing that made many women she worked with uncomfortable, it was asking them to talk authentically about why they were better than anyone else.

"WholeHeart is organic, it is bite sized, and it is low on the glycemic index while still tasting great."

Sophia had worked really hard on that differentiator, since Greg had told her just last month that they were absolutely going to need to raise capital to keep growing at their current rate. She really believed this about WholeHeart, too, but that didn't stop her voice from shaking.

"That's really strong, Sophia," said Ramona, and she meant it. "Tell me why you're getting a little shaky there."

"I think it's because there are lots of companies that can have that, right? Look at Hu Kitchen. Look at Mast. Even Hershey's has an organic line!" she scoffed. "How in the hootenanny does anyone successfully launch a product without gazillions of dollars today? You just get ripped off and kicked down."

Phoebe cracked up at "hootenanny," making a note to use it in her next Insta-story.

"Sophia, I want to talk to you about the concept of a brand differentiator. Because I think you're closer than you think.

"Think of a differentiator like a promise to your customers. The promise needs to be compelling to your customer, it must be authentic and credible, and no matter what, you must always keep your promise.

"It is very rare that you will be the *only* business in the world that offers these things. And I think what happens to women is we are so focused on being authentic that if we think for one moment we are promoting something that is not totally unique to us, then it is somehow not good enough."

"So you're saying we have to believe our own bullshit?" Hannah asked.

"Sort of!" said Ramona, laughing. "But your differentiator must be true. Remember, it needs to be true and important to your customer. And I've also got a tip to help you know that it's not bullshit."

Sophia's ears perked up. As far as she was concerned, her differentiator was both true and bullshit. Could they possibly understand what she meant by that? Like, WholeHeart *was* organic, bite sized, and low on the glycemic index. And if it didn't taste great, would people even buy them? But at the same time, she kept thinking about every competitor that could probably say the same thing.

"I want your differentiator to be able to be proven. When you are able to measure the proof points of your differentiator, it allows you to be more assured of what makes you *you*, and it allows you to stand by it in a deeper, more meaningful way. Plus, data helps you verify to the outside world that your promise can be kept."

"Not just to the outside world," said Phoebe. "To you, too." She looked at Sophia. "Hershey's can't say their shit is always bite sized, or organic. And you know what? It's tasty but that sugar count, though! Oof."

"You could do customer taste tests!" said Renee. "Have them taste different organic products and report on the study. I'll host them!"

"Or, you could launch new products every single year, committing to keeping them natural, bite sized, and low sugar!" Elena was excited for Sophia now. This was a road map she could support. If this business was applying for funding that required an essay, Elena would know *exactly* what to write to get her in.

Suddenly, Sophia realized that she had more than she thought when it came to her secret sauce. She just needed to lean into it and live up to it.

"All right, everyone! Since you're all so excited, let's do a group exercise. I chose Sophia here because I thought she had a strong secret sauce that could be expanded upon. But finding your secret sauce can be really difficult if you haven't worked on it. Let's see where you all fall on this spectrum. And remember, your secret sauce is *not* a slogan, so it doesn't have to be catchy. It has to be true, it has to be wanted by your customer, and it has to be able to be proven in some way." Ramona busted out her trusty easel and Post-it notes. "Everyone, let's see that secret sauce."

Dutifully, the women grabbed markers and Post-its, scribbled down their thoughts, then stuck them on the easel.

we find you the stylist that is perfect for you, guaranteed.

We have a great fitness program that is accessible to all????

NO. CLUE.

WholeHeart is organic, it is bite sized, and it is low on the glycemic index while still tasting great.

The only place for female artists to live their shared experiences.

I'm the best person to get your kid into the school they want to go to.

The best coffee in Omaha? I'm stuck!!!

Casey put her Post-it note below Renee's.

The #1 spot for communities to connect in town, while having delicious coffee.

"Okay, so these are a great start, and while you're not all quite there yet, I'm going to share with you two ways to work on your secret sauce. The first is top-down. You and your leadership team decide what you are going to commit to as a promise, and you build your company, your offerings, and your systems around that promise. That is sort of what most of you did here. You committed to what you *think* makes you different, and to what your customers want and need."

Ramona looked around the room. Wendy was nodding, Phoebe smiled, but most of the others looked unsure.

"But," Ramona continued, "there's also a bottom-up strategy. This is where you collect lots of data to create your secret sauce. Think of it like you're cooking a sauce to throw on your pasta. First, you throw in some customer feedback—finding out what your buyers say about why they buy your product or service is the first ingredient. Then you sprinkle on some feedback from your employees on what *they* think makes you special, for a little seasoning. Then you stir in looking at the positioning of competitors and the industry pain points.

"That will give you a healthy amount of what I like to call 'impasta' sauce . . . because you'll be looking at it, questioning yourself, and feeling like an imposter. Get it?" Ramona laughed, but the joke landed like a really heavy meatball. *Oh well, can't win them all.*

"So next, think about how you can prove it! Ways to prove your secret sauce: clinical tests, customer surveys, ingredient lists, quarterly reports . . . The ways are endless, really, but you have to incorporate this measurement into your company's processes and commit to them. This isn't just to overcome imposter syndrome, by the way. It's to keep your company focused, differentiated, and strategic."

"I have an idea!" said Renee. "Since the secret sauce is a promise, let's all promise one another that we will refine our secret sauces, and share them with one another one day! Pinky swear?"

Eight pinkies raised in the air and came together, in a collective promise that they swore they'd keep.

SECURE YOUR
SECRET SAUCE

As you see from our fable, it's not easy to find that je ne sais quoi—the *X* factor that makes your company better than anyone else's in the market. In the Whisper Way program, I call this your "secret sauce." Your secret sauce is a promise that you make, primarily to yourself, and commit to upholding in order to maintain a competitive advantage.

In this chapter, Ramona talks about the two ways to develop your secret sauce: the top-down method and the bottom-up method. Again, the top-down method is where you and your leadership team settle on what you *think* makes you unique and commit to that promise. The bottom-up method is a way of crafting your promise based on data from your users/customers, your employees, and even your competitors. Personally, when I developed the brand promise for Likeable, my social media agency, with my team, I used the bottom-up method. My leadership team all flew to sunny Florida in the cold winter months, committed to discovering exactly what made us better than every other agency out there.

We came armed with data. Prior to attending, we collected the following information:

- We interviewed key customers about what made us indispensable to them.
- We interviewed employees about what they thought we were the absolute best at and why.
- We researched competitor pitches and how they presented themselves.

We then looked for common themes. Our customers mentioned how fast we were, which we needed to be if we were delivering trending social media content. The other thing they mentioned was that they really felt we understood social media in a way that other agencies said they did, but didn't. And finally, we were just a pleasure to work with—and our name made that clear.

Our employees, meanwhile, thought we were great at delivering smart social media content quickly. And they loved the culture.

Our competitors had a lot of bright shiny campaigns on their sites, so it was clear that showcasing work was important, but it was more about the sizzle than proving any kind of promise. But we saw that the two areas they highlighted most were their team and their work, so we made note of that.

We also called up past clients, prospects, and connections in our industry that could be buyers, and we asked them one question: "What do you hate the *most* about working with agencies?"

The answer was pretty much unanimous: They hated being billed for useless hours and wasted time.

After a brief workshop, we came up with our brand promise:

We offer faster service, from the smartest in social, with likeability guaranteed.

We committed to measuring that promise by conducting biannual surveys of our clients and our employees. We also committed to an action if we didn't deliver on that promise. We would "take the time to make it right"—meaning we would not bill for any hours needed for something that didn't meet a timeline, or didn't take a social-first approach, or wasn't presented in a likeable way. We called that our likeable guarantee.

Speaking of billing for hours, we had another component to our secret sauce that differentiated us in a meaningful way. Clients hated overage hour billing. What if, instead, we priced by deliverable? This was the start of our Content Credit System, a pricing method that allowed us to have clients subscribe to "credits," which could be redeemed for "real-time content." A video would cost more credits than a tweet, so you subscribed to a certain number, and our team was able to plot out the amount of content they'd deliver each month based on the number of credits a client had. Also, it was much easier for our account team to talk about adding more credits versus spending more hours. This small switch, combined with the commitment to our brand promise, led to triple-digit revenue growth.

How can you find your secret sauce? Well, it needs to be true, to meet your customers' needs, and to be provable. And you want to be able to uniquely solve a pain point, just like I did with the Content Credit System. So let's make your secret sauce together, shall we?

FINDING THE RECIPE FOR YOUR SECRET SAUCE

Most good sauces—especially red sauces—start with tomatoes, onions, salt, and garlic.

> **Tomatoes = *Top* Customers:** Ask your customers, why do they buy what you sell? Why do they choose you over your competition? What do you think is your strongest attribute?

Onions = *O*wn Employees: Here you want to ask your employees what they love about working here, but you also want to dig into why they are most proud of what you sell. What makes it great? How are you better than others in your category in their eyes?

Salt = *S*ome Competitors: Here's where you want to look at competitors and evaluate what they are trying to say their own secret sauce is. Match it up against what your customers and employees say about you. If more than one of them are promising what you think makes you different, it's not a secret sauce. Dig deeper.

Garlic = *G*reatest Industry Pain Point: What is the thing that is plaguing your customer right now, and is there a way to solve it? Brainstorm some ideas.

The only way to know if sauce is cooked perfectly is to taste it. And the only way to know if your secret sauce is a true advantage is to measure it. As you write down your secret sauce, ask yourself, *How do I know this is true?* And if you can't quantify that answer, it's probably just marketing speak. By quantifying the answer, even in a light way (like surveys), you are not only standing by what makes you *you*, but you are giving yourself substance to back up the confidence you need in order to lead a growing company.

Tomatoes
Top Customers
Our customers choose us
because:

1.

2.

3.

4.

5.

Onions
Own Employees
Our team thinks our offerings
are great because

1.

2.

3.

4.

5.

Salt
Some Competitors

1.

2.

3.

4.

5.

Garlic
Greatest Pain Point to Solve

1.

2.

3.

4.

5.

Ways I will prove it:

My secret sauce is:

I can improve my customers' pain points by:

Remember: It is not so easy to find your secret sauce. If you don't find it right away, keep asking your customers and your employees. Keep reading about competitors you admire, and ask yourself what makes them different. Look at what problem the market has right now that you are uniquely equipped to solve. And remember to focus on measurement and proof points. Not only will it make your secret sauce more compelling, but it will help convince you that you are as good as you say you are, especially when you're in one of those low moments of entrepreneurship where you're questioning yourself.

REAL-LIFE
SECRET SAUCE

WHITNEY WOLFE HERD

These days, there are more than 1,500 dating apps and websites in operation around the world. But in 2014, the online dating scene was just beginning to become the booming market it is today. Tinder, in particular, was on the rise, with its users spending an average of 90 minutes per day on the app just two years after its inception. Things were humming along until one cofounder, Whitney Wolfe Herd, filed a sexual harassment lawsuit against Tinder and its parent company, IAC. Whitney was called a liar and a slut by her cofounders, and she produced text messages that showed them telling her that it was "slutty" for her to be a cofounder of a "hook up" app like Tinder. She claimed she was forced to resign because of a hostile work environment. The courts agreed, and six months later, Whitney founded Bumble, a new dating app based on a problem she wanted to help solve.

One could easily see that Bumble was built with a simple secret sauce: Women would feel in control, in an environment free of misogyny, where all relationships were equal. In an interview with *Forbes India*, Whitney said, "Bumble was actually born at a point when I wanted nothing to do with dating apps. Instead, I wanted to create a social network where women could exchange compliments. But then the idea became Bumble."

In her letter to Bumble members, she stated, "When I founded Bumble, it was because I saw a problem I wanted to help solve. It was 2014, but so many of the smart, wonderful women in my life were still waiting around for men to ask them out, to take their numbers, or to start up a conversation on a dating app. For all the advances women had been making in workplaces and corridors of power, the gender dynamics of dating and romance still seemed so outdated. I thought, what if I could flip that on its head? What if women made the first move, and sent the first message?"

Here's how Whitney delivered on this important differentiator while still building a relatively traditional dating app:

- On Bumble, women make the first move if it is a heterosexual match—a fundamental difference from any other dating app out there.
- After matching with someone, women have twenty-four hours to send a message before it disappears.
- Users can hide their first name or profile, and they can block, report, or un-match easily.
- The "private detector" feature detects and blurs any inappropriate image that is shared, and it alerts the user.
- The "photo verification" and "request photo verification" features give users a sample photo to pose and take a similar picture. Actual humans go through these verifications as an additional step and reject the image if it is not a match.

What differentiated Whitney's company also resonated with her employees. A study by Comparably revealed that Bumble's mission, vision, and values motivate 100 percent of Bumble employees.

On February 11, 2021, just seven years after starting the platform, Whitney took Bumble public, becoming the youngest female founder (yet!) to do so. And, to top it off, she was also a billionaire CEO *and* a new mom. A feature in *Forbes* reminds us that Whitney embodies the challenging of the status quo when building businesses: "We have to remind ourselves that the old rules of the working world were created by and for men, and make our own." In November 2023, Whitney stepped down as CEO of Bumble in order to "get back to her founder roots." Perhaps it was because she had achieved her mission of building something that tackled a need in the market that no one else was able to; despite the proliferation of dating apps, Bumble remains one of the strongest—the third most popular in the US, according to Pew Research. I look forward to seeing the next company Whitney works on, as I'm sure, based on Bumble, it will have a strong, defined, measurable secret sauce.

Chapter Eight
Perfect Your Profit

Man, were these women inspiring. Phoebe was furiously scribbling down all of her favorite gems from the retreat during the break. She was sitting on a porch swing when Ramona came and sat down next to her.

"Hello, friend," said Ramona. "I wanted to talk to you about something. Do you have a minute?"

"Sure," replied Phoebe, excited to be getting some individual attention.

"I think you're a total star, Phoebe. I think you're inspiring; I think you're a creative visionary. I think you're confident. And I think you have a strong idea with Be A Badass. I love the idea of a community of artist creators, and I *really* love the idea that you can teach them to be confident and make money."

Yes. Phoebe knew she had the stuff! And now Ramona was validating it! She felt seen!

"And, I think you're leaving a lot of money on the table. And that might impact your secret sauce. Because if you don't make money, how can they?"

Phoebe felt all of her confidence shatter into a million pieces. She wasn't good with feedback. Her wall of armor was her "I am the bomb" energy, and when someone poked it, it pissed her off. And yet, she knew that Ramona was right, and that, coupled with her impending student loans, led her to push past her own insecurity and fear of feedback.

"Really. So what would you do, Ramona?" She tried to get the bit of contempt she was feeling out of her voice, but there was just a twinge of it still there.

"Well, here's the thing, Phoebe. I want you to succeed, and I don't want you to run out of money doing it. I think it's great that you don't need much, but if you don't make at least what you need to live, your dream is at risk of being one of the 50 percent of small businesses that don't survive beyond five years."

"I'm trying to survive year one!" said Phoebe, finally letting her guard down.

"About a fifth of businesses don't even do that," said Ramona.

"Women-owned businesses?"

"Businesses, period. But the stats for women are truly abysmal. I'm not saying this to be all gloom and doom, but this is the reality right now. Women-owned businesses bring in barely 6 percent of all business revenues. Those numbers haven't changed since 1997, Phoebe. And the reason I'm talking to just you now is that I believe you have the confidence and the entrepreneurial spirit to go all the way—and if you're not profitable, you won't be able to sustain for the long haul."

"*Lord,*" said Phoebe, thinking, *How does anyone survive?*

"Okay, I'm going to advise you to do something that is sort of backward from the way most business coaches do anything. But the reason I do it this way is I know that this is what many women, even confident, bold, visionary women like you, need in order to grow, *especially* if they don't want to go out and raise money. I call it 'scrappy and happy.' When you are scrappy and happy, you are rejecting the norms of what we typically hear about with business success—which is almost always tied to going big and having investors believe in your business. I prefer a more realistic and practical approach."

Phoebe was really honored that Ramona was sharing this with just her.

"Phoebe, I want you to add up every expense in your life. Assume that the student loans hit, add in your rent, your groceries, utilities, and then think about what you need for fun money. Then add about 15 percent on top for savings money. Got it?"

Phoebe hated math generally, but that was pretty easy. Her expenses were about $5,000 a month all in. She knew 10 percent of $5,000 was $500, and she knew that half of that was $250, so $750 would be 15 percent. See, she didn't even need a calculator. Her monthly number was $5,750.

"You're going to think this is nuts, because it's not necessarily rooted in reality, but I want you to double the number now. That's going to account for taxes, and also allow for a fair amount of cushion."

Phoebe didn't need a calculator to know that that was $11,500.

"Now, multiply that number by twelve."

"All right, Ramona, I need my phone for that." Phoebe switched from her notebook to her phone and opened the calculator app. "It's $138,000."

"I like round numbers. Call it 140," said Ramona.

"Okay, I think I just threw up in my mouth a little," said Phoebe.

"When you're starting out, rather than worrying about your profit percentage, we are going to work backward to see how you can net the proper amount of profit. Since you're very small, and just starting out, I know you don't have staff."

"I have a virtual assistant!" said Phoebe.

"That's great!" said Ramona. "Now list out the expenses for the business, what you want to invest in this year. Give me an annual number for that one."

"It's actually not that much. I have my podcast producer, my CRM software, the hosting of the site. I'd say all in, we are looking at about $85,000 if I invested in some tech that I wanted, and maybe a few other little things."

"Well, it looks like we have our number! We would aim for your business to generate 225K annually—so you can pay your expenses and make the money you need to start saving."

Phoebe knew she should be confident, but she was scared. "It sounds like a lot."

Ramona knew this fear. The fear of a large looming number without any plan to get there. For Ramona, the numbers were in the eight-figure range when she was at her peak, but she also remembered the pressure when the numbers were smaller, and she didn't yet have scale. She thought she remembered that experience feeling significantly more overwhelming even though the numbers were so much smaller.

"Phoebe, I love this side of you. The squishy, vulnerable side. And honestly, I hope you use this side in your business: I think it makes you very relatable as a public face of the business! But let's break down the number. You're looking at roughly 19K a month of revenue. How can we get there?"

"Well, my four sources of revenue right now could be memberships, sponsorships, creator revenue, and events where I'm paid to speak or perform."

"Great! That's diversified, and even though some of it is reliant only on you for now, that's okay when you are starting out. Sometimes I think people are so focused on *scaling* that they decide to do the whole *work-on-the-business-not-in-the-business* thing too early."

"Oh, I've seen a million TikToks on that too."

"Yeah, TikTok is a lot of things, but you have to be careful not to fall down a rabbit hole of business influencers who talk about making millions in their sleep. There is no such thing as truly passive business income, and there's no get-rich-quick method that doesn't involve a lot of luck."

"Preach."

"All right," said Ramona. "You have four different methods of generating income. Are they all equal, or could some generate more than others?"

"Well, memberships are the goal, right? That's what builds me long-term. But I don't think I want to count on that revenue yet in a deep way. I want to make sure I give them enough value. For creator revenue, it's a simple math calculation. People pay me to create content for them based on how many followers I have, so while it's not a business on its own, I can predict it with relative ease. With speaking, I know I can make a lot because I'm known, and large corporations love to have entertainment at their events that feels different and meaningful. My spoken word does that. And sponsorships—well, I could probably test one for the community this year to start."

"Let's weigh those. It sounds to me like you could do 35 percent content revenue, 35 percent speaking revenue, 20 percent membership revenue, and 10 percent sponsorship revenue. Get that calculator out and tell me what that would mean in dollars for you."

Back Phoebe went to her phone:

Okay, so 35 percent of $225K was $79K. For creator content, at $7K per post, she was looking at one post a month. That was doable.

She made $75K last year from speaking, so she knew that would be doable for her.

This would leave her with 20 percent for membership revenue: $45K. It would be a stretch, but if she broke that down to about $4K a month, it was definitely possible.

And selling one of her corporate speaking clients for $20K seemed like something she could handle. They'd be the first sponsor—maybe they could sponsor the entire season of the podcast that she was launching next year.

"Yes, that feels doable. A lot of work, but doable. You know I know how to hustle, Ramona!"

"I do. But here's the thing. Even if you don't hit every one of these, you will hit enough to likely survive another day. That's the struggle, right? We've just gotta get through those first five years, and get to a steady revenue stream, and figure it out as we go. Ideally, we make your income less dependent long term on your speaking fees and personal social media, since having it be focused on the business versus just you is ideal for exit. But for now, this is a perfect, beautiful work in progress. It's like we are changing the tires on a moving vehicle!"

Phoebe wrote that down. That was for sure going in her next piece.

Just then, they heard the women gathering. It was time for the next session.

"Do you feel like you can be vulnerable enough to share what we did here, Phoebe?"

"Absolutely," said Phoebe. She couldn't wait to share what she had learned.

Exercise

PERFECT YOUR
PROFIT

This exercise is combined with some basic education around finance. If you're advanced in this area, feel free to skip it, but the last time I checked, most business owners don't go into business because they like accounting software. (Except maybe accountants? Sorry, accountants!)

I like to call this section "The Safe Girl's Guide to Being Scrappy and Happy." It's not rooted in science, nor financial theories. It doesn't account for investing, or interest, or anything that helps us make money in the long run. By the way, I strongly recommend that you learn about all of those things—pushing past a fear of money is a big passion point of mine, and I hope you learn about money early and often in your career. My tips for that are:

1. To understand business, read the *Wall Street Journal*. It's like Duolingo for finance, really. Once you become fluent in the common terms of finance, you'll understand so much more. (I first read this tip in Nicole Lapin's book *Rich Bitch*, and it was a game changer for me.)
2. Look to established female experts in this space for education around investing and budgeting. I *love* anything by Sallie

117

Krawcheck (CEO and cofounder of Ellevest), Nicole Lapin (finance journalist and TV anchor), Tori Dunlap (Founder of Her First $100K), and Tiffany Aliche (financial educator known as "The Budgetnista"). They all have newsletters, books, and podcasts, and their content is easily digestible.

3. When you don't understand something, google it, and recognize that there are many other people googling the same exact thing. Just make sure you're clicking on a trusted source (like any business publication, or sites like Investopedia), versus a rando with advice.

But back to my scrappy and happy guide to business. I started our business when my oldest daughter was three, and I was pregnant with my second. My husband was about to leave his teaching job to join me, but I wanted to make sure that we could at the very least make enough to pay for health insurance, something we'd be giving up once he left his job. It would be a bonus to also replace his salary, but primarily, I wanted to make sure I didn't have to have this new baby without proper healthcare!

At this point, I had very little business experience. I'd worked in marketing and sales but had never seen any kind of profit and loss statement (P&L) in my life. At the time, I didn't even have anyone in my network to go to who had done what I was about to do! I had no idea about profit margin or anything else.

Here's what I did.

I calculated how much I needed to pay for our expenses plus health insurance. I then doubled that number to account for what I called the three Ts—Taxes, Trust Fund (my tongue-in-cheek name for our savings), and Trouble—the unexpected stuff that comes up that you want to be prepared for.

I then separately looked at the operating costs for the business, making them as lean as possible and removing any form of salary that I was taking.

The two numbers, combined together, was what I needed the revenue to be in order for Dave to join me at Likeable, the first company we started.

I remember saying to Dave, "Okay, you want to join me? Find me a client that is $5,000 a month and we are there." He left his job at the end of the school year, the moment he hit the goal.

You might think that having a scrappier, bottom-up mentality (as opposed to setting big goals for the sake of growth) only works for solopreneurs who are just starting out. Let me tell you that I have used this method time and time again. When I sold my business to a larger company, I had an earnout, meaning that I had to hit both a revenue target and an EBITDA (profit) target over a three-year period. I was crushing the revenue numbers, but the margin was wavering a little bit, and I had to hit both to get to my target. And so, I busted out my scrappy girl guide, and started from the bottom.

How much did I need to make a month to hit the cumulative EBITDA target? And what amount of revenue would make it work from a percentage point of view, so I hit the amount I needed to deliver to the company at the percentage they needed? And by the way, even though I didn't need to, I still doubled my number for the three *T*s, just in case.

At that point, I had built an eight-figure business, I understood margin, I knew how profitable each of my projects were. But when there is a goal to hit where the stakes are high—whether it's surviving your first few years of business, hitting an earnout target, or building the company to prepare to sell—I always return to the basics.

Here's the formula. Try it!

THE SAFE GIRL'S GUIDE TO BEING SCRAPPY AND HAPPY

List your monthly living expenses.	Mortgage or rent: _____
	Utilities: _____
	Food and drink: _____
	Clothes and laundry: _____
	Household maintenance: _____
	Care costs (childcare or other): _____
	Transportation (gas, transit pass, etc.): _____
	Entertainment: _____
	Education: _____
	Other: _____
	Total: _____
Multiply monthly living expenses by 2 for TTT (Taxes, Trust Fund, and Trouble).	$\times 2 =$ _____ ($= A$)

List your monthly business operating expenses (do not include any salary for you).	This varies a lot depending on if you are a product business or a services business—but here are some of the basic categories: COGS (Cost of Goods sold): How much does it actually cost you to make what it is that you sell? Payroll: How much do your people cost? Operating Expenses: Your rent, office expenses, legal, accounting, and everything else generally falls into this category. _____ _____ _____ _____ **Total:** _____ (= B)
Add A and B together.	**A + B =** _____
Multiply by 12 for your annual goal.	**× 12 =** _____

How might you get to that number? Break it down by product or offering.	
If it's not feasible, set a plan:	
Could you pull back on expenses, either personal or business?	
Could you hit these numbers in 24–36 months?	
Are you open to fundraising?	

In addition to the scrappy approach, it's important that if you are a business owner, you know your numbers. The three documents you should really understand how to read are a Profit and Loss statement, a Balance Sheet, and a Statement of Cash Flows. For the purposes of understanding profitability in particular (the P in WHISPER), let's take a quick look at a P&L.

COMPONENTS OF PROFIT AND LOSS STATEMENT (ALSO CALLED AN INCOME STATEMENT)

P&Ls can look very different from industry to industry and business to business. Think: if your business sells products or services; if you have more than one type of income; if you have lots of operating expenses or very few. That said, they all have some basic components in common.

Revenue: Your company's sales.

COGS: Your Cost of Goods Sold. If you produce a product, what are the costs of the raw materials, the packaging, etc. If you run a services business, what are the costs of the employees needed to execute your services?

Gross Profit: The amount of income you have, less the money it costs to make it, is your gross profit. This is what you have left to operate the business, and make your profit.

Operating Expenses: These are the costs—whether administrative, general, and/or in sales—associated with keeping your business running during a specific time period. Think any rent you pay to maintain an office or warehouse, wages/benefits for staff, utilities, and supplies.

Operating Income: For the most part, operating income means your earnings before interest, taxes, depreciation, and authorization. Sound familiar? That's the artist also known as EBITDA. Note: EBITDA divided by your Gross Profit gives you your EBITDA percentage or EBITDA margin, which is something you'll be asked about if you talk to investors or acquirers. The higher your EBITDA percentage, the better.

Other Income and Expenses: On your P&L, this section covers unusual or infrequent income or costs—things that aren't related to your business's normal operations. This might include gains or losses from a sale of the company's assets, interest and dividend income from investments, and other occasional or nonstandard revenues or expenses. Taxes paid through the company can also go here as well.

Net Profit: This is the one you care about the most—because it is what you truly make after all is said and done. Your net profit is the amount you end up with after subtracting each and every expense.

If you feel embarrassed because you're not familiar with these terms, don't be—you aren't alone. Research conducted by Intuit Inc. found that more than 40 percent of small business owners identify as "financially illiterate." Remember my tips: Read the *Wall Street Journal*, find some experts you identify with, and don't forget that Google is your friend!

My single most important piece of advice on this is: Do not hide from your numbers, always have access to your accounting software, and, once you become fluent enough, set up the P&L the way it is easiest for *you* to read. (There are lots of ways to customize it!)

Action Item: Go into your accounting software and pull a P&L for your year to date. Do *not* ask someone to pull this report for you. If you don't know how, you can ask someone to walk you through how to do it, but you must know how to do it yourself—it is critical. Make sure you understand it, and ask whatever questions you may have of your bookkeeper. Do not be afraid, and keep going until you understand it easily.

REAL-LIFE
PROFIT

CAROLYN ARONSON

When you look at Carolyn Aronson now, you see a thriving Latina entrepreneur and philanthropist. She's made her reputation as the founder, CEO, and sole owner of one of just a few female-owned haircare brands worldwide.

But before she was the role model of many a young entrepreneur, she was, as she put it in an interview with *Forbes*'s "The One" series, "a poor starving hairdresser that was trying to just take the little bit of money I had and live off of it."

Carolyn was born into a large Puerto Rican family and was one of twelve children. At two weeks old, she was placed into foster care, and remained there until she was two years old, when she and one of her brothers were adopted into her family. Carolyn viewed her father as a pivotal reason that she was able to be successful as an entrepreneur. In the *Forbes* interview, Carolyn shared how her father taught her the basics of business, even though he himself was never an entrepreneur. "He thought I was crazy for wanting to be an entrepreneur, but he was extremely smart and supportive in what it was that I wanted to do and really gave me the tools to do it in a safe and good way." She continued, "He really showed me how to be my own little business at a very, very young age."

If her father was never an entrepreneur, how did he teach her the skills that she largely credits for her success? By teaching her the basics of finance. In the same interview, she recounts stories of daddy–daughter evenings spent at tax seminars and learning Quicken, money management software to manage personal finances. At eight years old, Carolyn opened her own checking account. As an adult, she learned how to do her own taxes. This goes back to my point from the exercise about the importance of becoming financially literate. You don't need to have a dad like Carolyn's to bolster your own financial skills and savvy! You don't need to become a pseudo-accountant to get more familiar with your finances. You simply need to commit to not avoiding them.

Carolyn founded her business, It's a 10, with her then-partner, Scott Scharg, in Detroit, Michigan. The idea behind the business was simple. In an interview with IdeaMensch, she talked about how, as a hairstylist, she had to use so many different products to suit different types of hair. As an entrepreneur, she set out to solve that problem. "I envisioned a line that was for everyone and delivered full, salon-quality results in just one bottle . . . The entire premise of the line is that every product offers ten benefits in one and works on ALL hair types—no guesswork, and always instant results."

As the company grew, Carolyn and Scott started realizing that they had severe creative differences. In 2015, they agreed they couldn't keep working together and decided to sell the company, but they couldn't find a suitable buyer. Carolyn realized the only solution was for her to buy out Scott. But It's a 10 had grown so much, the valuation was higher than any number she could have imagined self-financing. Carolyn used those early lessons on money management and profitability to self-finance the acquisition through the profits of the company. It took her two years to figure out that she was ready to make the offer. Meanwhile, Carolyn told *Inc.* magazine, "The company was starting to go through some turbulent times because we both were just really ready to get away from each other . . . The best thing for the life of the company was for one of us to buy the other out."

In 2017, Carolyn Aronson took on seven figures of debt to purchase It's a 10 from her cofounder at a nine-figure value. Today, according to *Forbes*, It's a 10 boasts nearly a billion dollars in annual retail sales, and Aronson is completely debt-free. In December 2023, Aronson decided to step into the buy side of acquisitions, as It's a 10 acquired hair regrowth company Nisim to fold into the company and accelerate growth.

Carolyn told *Forbes*, "I'm an independently owned company, I'm a self-funded company, with an extremely solid foundation. . . I use the tools that (my father) taught me every single day." Carolyn is a perfect example of perfecting profit, which has enabled her to make choices like funding acquisitions and living an incredible lifestyle. When and if she finally does sell It's a 10, it will be because she wants to, and not because she has to.

Chapter Nine

Elevate Your Executive Team

As the women returned to their seats, Phoebe animatedly filled them in on the scrappy and happy model. She saw a lot of them scribbling their own finances in their notebooks. If the women responded this positively to that exercise, Phoebe felt certain that her community of artists on her platform would benefit from it as well. She was feeling on top of the world.

Ramona called them to attention. "This is our last exercise before lunch. We will then have a short afternoon exercise, a break, and then dinner with a concluding activity. In the morning, you all can head out on your way to embrace the greatness I know in my heart that you were each born to achieve."

A collective air of anxiety filled the room. "How are we going to do all of this on our own when you're gone?" Renee asked.

"You all can rely on your teams. You need to trust the teams that you've built to carry out the plans that you set here," Ramona said calmly.

"That's easy for everyone else," said Elena. "I don't have a team. When a kid needs help, it's me who handles it. When a parent has a question, it's me who answers it. When an essay needs tweaking, it's me who edits it. It is all me."

"And are you happy that way?" said Ramona, who already knew the answer but was just waiting for Elena to find it.

"Well, I'm sure as hell happy not to have to answer to anyone else. And I definitely need a lot of control in my life. And since work is pretty much my whole life, I don't mind how much time it takes up. But there are two things that are nagging at me since being here."

"And they are . . . ?" prompted Ramona, knowing she was getting closer.

"Well, the first is obviously, what if I get hit by a bus? And for me, that had me thinking about all of my clients. What would they do? I started thinking about competitors of mine, but my clients would not do as well with them, because my process feels so bespoke and different from anyone in the market. So I started thinking, if I could teach others to do what I do like I do it, then maybe I'd have something much bigger and much more meaningful on my hands."

"Interesting!" Ramona said. She knew she'd have to tread carefully with Elena, who was tough as nails and never wanted to feel pushed by anyone to do anything. The idea had to feel like her own.

"So, let's say you needed to replicate yourself, and, as you said, teach others to do what you do. What would you need?"

"Well, I want to focus on my client work. First, I'd need someone to literally follow me around and document my process. Because it's all in my head and there's no way in hell I'm sitting down to write it all out. I work on essays all day; I can't work on that. I would then need to turn that into an instruction manual, I suppose. And then I'd need someone to go out and find people who could be me. To do that,

I would need to really think about what makes me *me*, you know? And then really be particular about that. And then we'd have to make sure that we have enough business for all these mini-mes, so I'd need to know that they could actually bring us students; I guess I'd have to document that process too."

"Sounds like you had a lot of the answers all along, it was just deciding you wanted to do it. But I know you, Elena. You talked about how you had a year's worth of your salary saved before you left your job. Are you prepared to invest in this?" Ramona asked. She wanted to challenge Elena just a little bit, in the hope that she'd lean in. From the look on Elena's face, it looked like it worked.

"Well, considering I've been a single woman making bank for twelve years now, I think I'm just fine, Ramona! But I think the thing that I'd start with is hiring the person who is going to document everything. I don't think I am ready for another me just yet. Heck, I don't think the world is ready for another me!" she laughed, bouncing back from being pissed about any implication that she wouldn't lean in.

"You joke, but that's actually more important than you think!" replied Ramona. "One of the biggest mistakes founders make is to hire people just like them. After all, we tend to value the best qualities we see in ourselves. But really, we want to hire people with skills that complement ours. Elena, your skills clearly lie in servicing your clients, impeccable essay writing, and sales—otherwise you wouldn't be the size you are all by yourself. Is that right?"

"You bet your bippy it is," said Elena.

"Okay, so if those are your skill sets, what are the things you spend your time on that do not fall into the realm of your own superpowers?"

"Billing, documentation, details beyond the details of a really well written essay, gosh, I could go on."

"Okay, so it might be easy just to hire for that for now, right? But as you grow, you'll want someone who excels in those areas—which sound more process oriented—*and* has some qualities that will allow them not just to be your order taker but to actively contribute to the business, right? Otherwise, you could just hire a virtual assistant and call it a day!"

Elena hadn't thought of it that way. "*Should* I just hire a virtual assistant? What do you think?"

"I think you need to go back to the why, Elena. You said that the reason was twofold. First, it was to make sure your clients were served if you were hit by a bus, and the second was to create a model where you could create more yous. I think either way it's clear that no matter what, you don't want things to stay the same. So you have to decide if you want to *delegate*, or you want to *scale*. Delegation is a very important skill, one that you can and should develop, whether it's with a virtual assistant, a high-level executive assistant, or even a bookkeeper. But scaling requires not just hiring around your skill sets. It involves hiring people who will push you. It involves people who might be smarter than you."

Ramona paused to watch Elena's reaction.

"Nobody's smarter than this queen!" said Hannah, breaking the tension just a bit. The room erupted into laughter, which turned into full-on howls. Hannah figured they needed that.

The room quieted, and Elena spoke.

"Do you think I'm scared to scale because I want to feel like the smartest person in the room?"

"Do you?" asked Ramona, ever so gently.

"I'm not sure if that was true, but if it was, it can't be for a minute longer. I know what I have to do. I have to hire someone who has complementary skill sets, but someone badass and brilliant who will challenge me and help me build this thing the way I want it!"

The ladies couldn't help it—they all started clapping. You could see that they were genuinely all so happy for Elena.

"This is truly wonderful work, Elena. I have only one piece of advice for you, if you're open to it?" Ramona was still treading lightly.

"Sure!" said Elena. She felt like she had worked through a major roadblock in her life just now, and she wasn't ready to stop.

"When you're hiring, for your first hire and any hire, I want you to think about what skills you need for the role, and we talked about that. But I also want you to think about your values. Often at a company, we call these core values, but since it's just you right now, I want you to think about what *you* value at work. What are your values when it comes to the company you want to build. And make sure when you're hiring people with different skills, you're hiring people with the same core values in business that you want the company to represent."

"So you're saying, look for people that are hardworking, honest, and have a deep desire to win? Like me?"

"Yes! Or, as you would say—You bet your bippy!"

"Done," said Elena. And she meant it, too.

ELEVATE EXCEPTIONAL
EXECUTIVES

Your business is neither scalable nor sellable if it is entirely reliant on you. Over the course of my career, I have found hiring and leading people to be the hardest part of scaling a company. As someone who ran an agency where people *were* the product, I read countless management books on how to develop high-performing teams. Ultimately, the thing I found the most valuable was to be extremely methodical and discerning when it comes to hiring and cultivating your leadership team. When you are evaluating potential partners or key hires, I want you to look at the three *C*s: Core Values, Competencies, and Collaboration.

- **Core Values:** Company values are the fundamental beliefs and principles that guide the organization. They are the beliefs you hold to be true, and they give employees a sense of purpose—something that, according to a McKinsey & Company survey, 70 percent of executive employees said they find through their work.

- **Complementary Competencies:** When building your executive team, you want to make sure that there's not a deep doubling up on skill sets, especially on a lean team. So while the values should be similar or aligned, the competencies should be diverse.

- **Collaboration:** Scaling a company is not always full of unicorns and rainbows. Quite frankly, it can be a bit of a slog. It's going to involve a lot of tough conversations, disagreements, and difficult choices. Is the person going to push you, and collaborate with you on the decisions you need to make to get to a common goal? Will they offer a fresh perspective? This is an important area because you don't want a pushover, and you also don't want a steamroller. You want a collaborator—someone who is going to bring the best of themselves to work with you.

There's another C-word that is commonly used, that I want you to consider carefully before using it. That *C* is "culture." The word *culture* is often radically misused, and I know I have made this mistake in my own career. For most of my time at Likeable, we hired "for culture." Culture fit is when an individual's attitude seems like it aligns with the organizational culture—its values, work environment, and traditions. By that logic, hiring for supposed "culture fit" can often be at odds with any diversity, equity, and inclusion efforts. We are drawn to people that we have things in common with, creating what's called an "affinity bias." While I believe that fitting into a company's culture is usually a good thing, I think *adding* to a company's culture is a much better thing. It goes beyond diversity (though that's important on its own). Consider: Will a prospective executive hire bring different viewpoints? Different experiences? Could their different ideas or background be an asset, for instance if they could help you to innovate or create a new service or product offering?

And, since I'm a big fan of both cookies and alliteration, I present you a delicious dessert to follow your RED wine and your special sauce: *C* is for cookies (and core values, and competencies, and collaboration, and culture). When talking to your next potential exec, consider the following:

BUILD AN EXCEPTIONAL EXECUTIVE TEAM

List Your Core Values. Does this person share them and can they demonstrate examples from their past that showcase them? For every example, carve out a bite of this part of the cookie!

Competencies: Write out the skills you need in an executive for this role. Match them up to the experiences of the prospective executive. If it's a match, celebrate with a bite of this cookie!

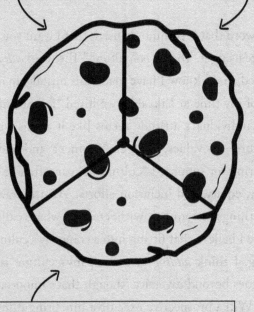

Could this person *add* to your culture? Look for how their differences might complement the current culture. If it works, wash down that cookie with some milk!

Collaboration: Ask the potential hire about examples of when they disagreed with an approach of a leader, and how they handled it. Ask about a time that they were aligned with someone on an end goal but didn't agree on the path to get there. Good answer? This part of the cookie is yours.

I want to add one more point here. I have many friends who are consultants or single-person operations and truly want to stay that way. If that is your choice, and it is intentional, I'm here for it. However, if you want your business to be transferrable in any capacity whatsoever, you want to make sure that your processes and thinking are, like Elena planned for post-retreat, totally documented. If this is the case for you, you have my permission to retitle the E in Whisper from your "executives" to your "ecosystem." Every bit of that ecosystem must be written down. Otherwise, your business will not only be unsellable, it will be unmanageable for anyone other than you.

REAL-LIFE
EXECUTIVE
TEAM

STEPHANIE NADI OLSON

After ten years in her role in advertising, Stephanie Nadi Olson was burnt out. She was making a ton of money, but with two young children, one of whom was still breastfeeding, she did not feel like the working world was built for her. Said Stephanie on Inc.'s *What I Know* podcast, "It's just unsustainable . . . when you are a caregiver for your children, or your parents, or anybody else." She had an inkling that she might not be alone in that thought, so in 2018, Stephanie launched We Are Rosie—creating a platform for remote work in marketing. The platform matched at-home marketing professionals with contract jobs at large organizations, many of which Stephanie was connected to through her tenured career in advertising.

Before starting We Are Rosie, Stephanie's career was primarily in ad sales. Sales is often a solo sport, and prior to this venture, she had been a "people manager" for less than a year. "I feel like I've gotten my MBA in leadership about a hundred times over since I launched the business," Stephanie wrote in a letter to her online community. Selling is only one piece of running a company, while managing people is a whole other ballgame. And yet, in a five-year timeframe, Stephanie built a team that developed a marketplace that would receive a nine-figure valuation.

How does one go from being a lone wolf to building a team that can accomplish that kind of feat? Stephanie credits much of the growth of We Are Rosie to her executive team and her advisory board, whom she describes as "people who have decades more leadership experience" than she did. She continues, "I made up for my own lack of formal leadership experience with theirs, and . . . it helped me form my own leadership style quickly."

As the team grew, the leadership team changed and evolved. I spoke to Stephanie about this on my podcast, *The Exit Whisperer.*

She told me, "We went from zero to fifty employees in just a few years. And I knew very early I needed to hire for my weaknesses and just set these people free and they know they can always come home to me if they need guidance or overall strategy, information, or vision, but truly, when the company is growing like this, I've got to just trust. As a control freak, a perfectionist, and a type-A, that was a big deal for me—and it paid off in spades. I hired really good people and they were smart and capable and driven."

Another decision she made about her leadership team, and the employees at We Are Rosie, was to make it less hierarchical, and more about outcomes than about people management. She told me, "There are so many incredible leaders on my team that do not manage a team. This idea that leadership only shows up when you have responsibilities for direct reports is as old-school as the forty-hour, year-round workweek we're seeking to disrupt at We Are Rosie. It relies on the idea of a hierarchical career path—that the only way to reach new heights at work is to literally 'move up' the org chart. So many people aren't interested in that. And judging by how many terrible people managers exist, not everyone is suited to do it either. I am thankful for the people on my team who've decided to lead as individual contributors. I am thankful we have a culture that allows them to be heard, their thoughts respected, and for them to have a career path that isn't strictly up and to the right. Find and embrace these leaders in your organization early and often."

Having the right team and combining it with the right product worked, and it worked fast. Less than five years into growing the company, We Are Rosie established itself as "the flexible talent marketplace for the advertising and marketing world," as described in a press release. With over ten thousand independent marketers, We Are Rosie helped companies like Bumble, Meta, IBM, and Microsoft fill their marketing needs with top talent. All the while, We Are Rosie provided that talent with weekly pay and benefits. In 2021, just five years after the idea came into her head, the company received an infusion of capital valuing the company at $110 million, but not before Stephanie bootstrapped it with contracts from more than twenty-five *Fortune* 500 brands and six major advertising holding companies.

After five years of incessant work on the startup, and achieving an incredible valuation, Stephanie was ready to step out of the CEO role and into the Executive Chair of the Board role, slowing her pace for the first time in fifteen years. She couldn't have done it without building a core, competent, collaborative executive team.

REAL-LIFE
ECOSYSTEM

MAGGIE LORD

I know, we usually only show one real-life example per tenet. But in my work, I come across a ton of solopreneurs, and when we get to the executive team section, they cringe. Just like I spoke about at the end of this implementation portion, many of them (and perhaps many of you!) have no intention of ever hiring a full-time employee. But can they still build a sellable business? Absolutely!

Maggie Lord built and scaled content site Rustic Wedding Chic, and sold to David's Bridal, the world's largest bridal retailer, without ever hiring a single full-time employee.

Maggie launched in 2008, just as the "rustic farmhouse wedding" trend was becoming popular. Her site featured DIY ideas for rustic weddings, along with wedding planning tips, inspiration, and an advice column on wedding planning. Maggie also diversified her revenue by building a directory of wedding vendors.

In the beginning, Maggie was like most solopreneurs, with the company's processes living in her head. But about five years into the business, she realized that needed to change. "It struck me that if something happened to me, no one would even be able to log in to the backend of the website." She slowly began to build out standard operating procedures. However, it was not until she was planning a maternity leave with her second child that she got super serious about ensuring the business could run without her. "That moment in time pushed me to create more structured, checklist-style procedures to ensure parts of the business could run without me."

As Maggie began to think about an exit, she became even more focused on establishing solid processes to ensure the company could thrive beyond her involvement.

She wanted to start with the areas that she considered the backbone of the company's success, creating end-to-end processes for creating editorial content, managing and publishing social media, overseeing the wedding vendor directory, and setting clear guidelines for brand partnerships and advertisers. But as a solopreneur, how might she accomplish that?

The first step Maggie took to make her company more transferable was to stop gatekeeping information. She began sharing with contractors not only how but why she made certain decisions for the business. By letting go of control—something that's easy to cling to as a solo entrepreneur—she gradually became comfortable with delegating and transferring her knowledge and skills.

The next step she took was creating checklists for various tasks, which initially served as simple onboarding documents for new contractors. These checklists later proved invaluable during the sale process.

Finally, she developed a detailed plan for future expansion. This plan outlined how the company could generate new revenue streams, expand the brand, and introduce additional product offerings.

"Since so much of the brand's success stemmed from my vision, I felt it was crucial to share a five-year overview of my strategies and ideas—essentially a deep dive into my thought process and what I would do with the company if I were still at the helm," said Maggie.

In February 2020, just before COVID hit, Maggie made a cold call that would change her life. With all of her procedures in place, she reached out directly to Jim Marcum, the CEO of David's Bridal. He took the meeting, and over the next several months, in the midst of the pandemic's total upheaval of the wedding industry, Maggie was able to negotiate a fantastic exit to David's Bridal.

Chapter Ten

Refine Your Roar

The group broke for lunch, which was served in four picnic baskets, each containing the freshest food from the farm and adorable blankets. "Try to connect with someone you haven't spent a lot of time with one-on-one on this trip," urged Ramona. She then asked Ivy to join her so they could talk agency life, and Ivy couldn't have been more thrilled.

"Hey, Mom?" said Casey, rather tentatively. "Wanna eat together? We haven't talked much on this trip." She wasn't sure if Renee would want to eat with someone else, considering Ramona's request.

"Does a bear shit in the woods? *Of course* I'll eat with you!"

Ever since Casey had gone off to college, Renee had lost a bit of the pep in her step. As much as Coffee+ was her identity, Casey was her whole world. They were the consummate *Gilmore Girls* mother-daughter duo, and when Casey moved to the East Coast for college, Renee had to fight the urge to follow her with every ounce of her being. She had done a good job separating and was determined not to be codependent. But there was no way on earth she was turning down an opportunity to picnic with her favorite human on earth.

Casey laid out the patterned blanket and started setting up the picnic. She was prepared to have a tough conversation.

"Mom?"

"Yes?" From her tone, Renee didn't know if Casey was going to tell her she was getting married, joining the Peace Corps, or starring in a film. She was that type of kid—she just tried everything and anything and it always seemed to work itself out. Renee was glad she got that gene from her father, because it definitely didn't feel like it was within her. She braced for whatever crazy idea from Casey was next, and was, as usual, both terrified and thrilled to hear about her adventures. But it turns out, Casey only had a question for Renee.

"Why don't you believe in yourself, Mom?"

Renee didn't know what to say. "You think I don't believe in myself? I supported us on my own, I built a great shop, where people love to gather. I paid your way through college. You have to believe in yourself to do that, Casey. Of course I believed in myself."

"I just wish you saw what I see, Mom. You are such a star. And the shop is amazing. Why are you afraid of that stupid new Starbucks, and why couldn't we, I mean you, consider growing bigger instead of shrinking?"

"Casey, I already told you, I don't want to put you in a situation where you'd have any debt."

"Mom. I already went to college. The house is paid for. Why can't we just take a chance?"

"*Enough!*" said Renee. Her safety was being challenged, and for the first time in a long time, her daughter was making her very anxious.

"Can I just share an idea with you that I had? It could be nuts, but it is something I wanted to share with you." Casey could tell she probably already had reached the limits of her mother's comfort.

Renee paused and took some of the cheese and crackers from the basket. Her stomach was fluttering—but from nerves or hunger she couldn't tell.

"Okay."

"Bear with me here. Coffee+ is known in our small town. But it's not really a brand that we worked on. It's a brand that evolved. I had an idea for a brand. I was thinking, Coffee MD."

She drew a little logo with a stethoscope on her napkin.

"It's not the coffee that's the medicine. It's the connections we make. It's the communities we serve. And of course, MD also stands for mother-daughter."

Renee couldn't help but smile.

Feeling bolder, Casey continued. "My idea is, we would rebrand and run the first Coffee MD. And maybe we could find other mother-daughter duos to start their own Coffee MDs. That's like a franchise, I think? We could always offer one up in a similar small city once we prove out that the marketing is powerful. I've been taking a lot of marketing classes, and I think your story, and one day our story, could be something special."

That Casey. Suddenly, her daughter's entire childhood flashed before Renee's eyes. When she wanted money to buy the latest trending toys, she opened a lemonade stand in order to pay for them. In high school, she played her guitar at the coffee shop for tips. When Renee dropped her off at college, she walked into the dorm not knowing a soul. When she backpacked through Europe and her cell phone stopped working, she figured out how to get back to her hostel just fine, and she even learned how to communicate with the local cell-phone shop owner who spoke zero English to get it fixed. She was resourceful. She was fearless. She had nothing to lose. Casey was all things abundance, while Renee felt like she herself had a scarcity mentality. And why shouldn't she? It served her well all these years. Now, in her forties, she had *so* much to lose. But she also knew she had experience. She could execute a plan set by someone fearless. Maybe they were the perfect pair. *Hmm, Coffee MD . . .*

"We'd have to invest in branding, we'd need a new website, we'd need new mugs . . ."

Casey let out a squeal. *"You'll really try this with me!?"*

"Yes, you maniac," Renee said. "As long as we have each other, we have nothing to lose, and everything to gain."

"I CAN'T WAIT TO TELL RAMONA!" yelled Casey.

She didn't have to wait long. Like the ethereal freak that she was, Ramona appeared exactly at the right moment. "How's it going, ladies?"

Casey excitedly shared her plans, and Renee seemed equally enthusiastic, if slightly more cautious.

"My friends," said Ramona, "this is a fantastic idea. But it's going to challenge you. You're going to need to take risks. You'll likely need capital. You'll need to push for press, you'll need to market not just the business, but you'll need to market an entire franchise. You'll need to do . . . well, a lot. It's going to require a level of ferocity that is not just innately within you—it's a practice that is a learned skill over time, and it's going to be really tough for someone who has been so risk averse. And so, I want to ask you two brave, bold lionesses a question. Are you ready to roar?"

Ramona put her hand out, face down.

Renee put her hand down on top of Ramona's.

Casey put her hand on top of Renee's.

"We're all in," said Renee.

"And what happens when you start to get afraid, and doubt yourself, and want to backtrack?"

"Well, we will want to look at the numbers, and evaluate, and consider." Renee felt an urge to pull her hand back from this high-five huddle they were in, but she stopped herself. "We push forward with a roar, Ramona. That's what we do."

Ramona nodded, feeling fulfilled and so appreciative of Renee's hard work to push past her fear.

"Let's roar," said Casey.

And with that, the three women let out a collective, excited, bellowing scream.

They were really going to do this.

"What is going *on* out there!?" Elena's voice reached them from inside the house. The three looked at each other and grinned.

"I'm glad you asked, Elena," Ramona called back. "Just sharing a collective *roar* out here—which is going to be the subject of our last lesson. Renee, Casey, if you wouldn't mind sharing . . . ?"

And with that, the nine ladies gathered for the final official activity of the weekend.

REFINE YOUR
ROAR

Welcome to the softest skill of the Whisper Way, which is therefore often the most difficult one to master. Renee struggles with it, just as so many real-life entrepreneurs do. In fact, when it comes to confidence, sometimes even I have trouble teaching it!

Whenever I think about confidence, I think about the game of tennis. My husband is a fantastic tennis player who has been playing for many years. He is excellent, and he is a ferocious competitor. I spent my high school years in theater and didn't have an athletic bone in my body. Before we got married, we were friends, and I remember he once took a date to go play tennis and proceeded to completely dominate. Needless to say, when he said he would love it if I learned to play, I was terrified.

The first thing I did was take a few lessons. I felt it was important to establish what I called *minimum viable confidence*. I learned the basic strokes, and how to volley a bit.

I showed up for my tennis date with my husband in the world's cutest tennis outfit. I even wore a visor embroidered with "I play for love"—ironic, of course, because that was my score throughout the first set.

My husband takes no prisoners on the court. Not even a wife in a goofy visor will be spared.

Immediately, massive anxiety set in. Thoughts of how badly I sucked filled my head. Shame around my lack of athletic skill, regret over never playing sports as a kid, and embarrassment around thinking that a lesson or two was enough to make me competent.

It was time to start the second set. I collected my thoughts. As I got up to serve, I started thinking about how these negative thoughts served me. Did they help me in any way? At all? I couldn't think of any benefit to thinking I wasn't good enough. I decided to reframe:

You are a badass with a great hat and you belong here. And you are going to get this serve in, and we are going to have a nice little rally. And you probably won't win, because Dave is an experienced tennis player, but you are going to get your shots in, mama. Now hit that ball.

When I pumped myself up and believed in myself, I performed better. And I'm not alone. Research consistently shows that our mindset affects our performance, and that there is real power in positive thinking and self-talk. Here are a few examples:

A study from 2020 found that, for athletes and people playing sports, positive self-talk motivates and helps them improve performance.

A recent study out of Stanford University found that having a positive attitude was just as relevant as a kid's IQ in predicting how they'd perform on math problems.

A study from 2019 found that students who gave themselves a pep talk with self-affirming statements had less performance anxiety before giving a speech, compared to those who didn't.

Here's another fun fact about positive self-talk. Talking to yourself using second-person pronouns rather than first-person pronouns (that is, calling yourself "you" instead of "I" or "me") can help you maintain a sense of calm, even when feeling anxious. A 2019 study in the *Journal of Sports Sciences* backs this up: Those researchers found that athletes who used second-person pronouns in their positive self-talk performed better.

When you are in a space where you are speaking negatively to yourself or questioning your own abilities in your entrepreneurial journey, I want you to do two things:

First, I want you to make sure that you do, in fact, have the minimum viable competence to tackle something. And if you don't, go get it. Just like I took my tennis lessons, and like we'll see in the "Real-Life Roar" section of this chapter.

Second, I want you to recognize when you are having these thoughts. I would like you to ask yourself, *How are these thoughts serving me right now? Are they helping me in any way?*

And then, I want you to try and give yourself a little pep talk. Try it in the second person—"you are" versus "I am." I promise it makes it easier.

Another thing I learned while playing tennis was timing. When my instructor Robin was teaching me, she would comment every time the ball came my way. "Bounce. Swing." Each time. "Bounce. Swing." I found myself learning timing through "bounce, swing," and long after she stopped saying it, I heard the timing in my head. And what I realized through "bounce, swing" was that I had more time than I thought to react to the ball. It felt like poetry—I'd hit it over, she'd hit it back. Bounce. Swing. The rhythm of it felt like a dance. The ball would come my way, and my racket would be back, waiting for it. It would bounce, with a short moment of silence, and then I would hit it back to my opponent.

The timing of bounce, swing was different with Robin than it was with Dave. With Robin, it was much slower, because she was trying to teach me and not trying to win. With Dave, the shots came fast, and I had to react quickly. But there still was the rhythm of bounce, swing, and there still was way more time than I thought when the ball came my way. There was still that brief pause of nothingness before the smack of the racket sent the ball back toward Dave, just like there was with Robin.

This made me think a lot about negotiations. When you get to a point where you want to sell your business, chances are, you are going to be negotiating in a room with mostly men. And since selling a business is one of the biggest decisions you'll make in your life, it's probably going to feel pretty scary. So whether you're negotiating for an eight-figure exit like I was, or you're negotiating for a contract with a client, I want you to remember the art of bounce, swing.

The person is going to say something.

It's going to fly your way and land.

And when it does, the best thing you can do is be prepared, and then pause, and then respond.

There is never, ever, a need to rush.

There is never, ever, a need to overexplain.

You are going to treat every negotiation as if you are listening to bounce, swing.

And if you combine that with positive thinking about your performance before you swing? Then you'll really win the game.

Ask yourself, "How do these negative thoughts serve me?"

THE ART OF BOUNCE, SWING

Tennis	Negotiations
Opponent hits your way.	Other person speaks.
Get in position, racket back.	You listen fully.
The ball bounces on your side of the court, you take a breath and time the swing.	You take a beat, think about the response, and then sit quietly for a beat.
Swing (hit it over to your opponent's side).	Respond thoughtfully.

And when you feel negative thoughts start to creep in, ask yourself: *How do these negative thoughts serve me?*

I want you to practice this in the next conversation you have today, even if it's not a negotiation, and see how it goes. Does the timing help you be more confident? What about hyping yourself up? Keep trying it until you feel a real difference.

REAL-LIFE
ROAR

MELISSA ROGNE

Even as a child, Melissa Rogne seemed to have an unlimited bounty of confidence and persistence. Never taking no for an answer, she was always described by her mother as "unstoppable."

It makes sense that she was able to sell her single-location aesthetic center, Rejuv, based in Fargo, North Dakota, to The Aspen Group, one of the largest and most trusted retail healthcare business support organizations in the United States.

Melissa had no intention of becoming an entrepreneur. On an episode of my podcast, *The Exit Whisperer*, she told me, "It was never about . . . 'I'm gonna build this multimillion-dollar empire.' It started with just wanting to have a really cool place to go to work."

She opened Rejuv Medical Aesthetic Clinic in 2005, with a focus on making beauty fun. Her mission was to empower everyone to discover their own personal beauty narrative.

In the beginning Melissa did it all. "When I started, I was the front desk, I was the practitioner, I was the accountant, I was HR, I was maintenance, you name it," she says. And that included what

Melissa described as her Achilles' heel, finance. She had never seen a P&L statement before, let alone run one.

Melissa had to bolster her inner confidence and enrolled in a financial literacy course to help her through. Because there weren't many aesthetic spas in the early 2000s, she signed up for a course based on financial literacy for salons. "I figured, eh, close enough! I think what is most important is knowing that you have the capability to learn. We have the capability to learn, we can do those hard things." She learned just enough to have enough competence to match her unwavering confidence, and she was off to the races.

Rejuv quickly grew to become the largest clinic in the Midwest, and it was ranked as an Allergan Top 100 clinic. Melissa knew that she was on to something as she grew from a staff of two to a staff of fifty, but she was always cautious never to overextend herself. She now had two young children and a lot more to lose, so she was intentional about growing methodically.

However, when she was asked to speak on a MedSpa success panel at an industry conference, she decided to attend, and speak, even though it felt out of her comfort zone. She told me, "I thought to myself, *Oh gosh, do I want to get on stage in front of all my peers?* You say yes. You get yourself out there. You push past the discomfort and you do it."

It was at this Vegas conference where she met an executive from The Aspen Group. He was looking to acquire a majority stake in a MedSpa chain with fifteen to twenty locations. Melissa, of course, had stayed intentionally small with one location. Still he approached her. "I remember it so clearly. He came up to me after seeing me speak on the panel and he said, 'I'd love to talk to you about your plans with Rejuv.' And I just smiled and said, 'Well, I'm headed to the exhibit hall. So if you would like to carry my bag, you can walk with me and talk with me while I sit in the exhibit hall.' I was trying to be funny. When he was like, 'Sure, I would love to walk and talk with you,' I knew something was going on!" When nothing immediately occurred after their walk and talk, Melissa assumed it was because she was too small, but hey, at least she went for it! Until one day, she got a call from the executive, letting her know that The Aspen Group founder and CEO was flying in to meet her.

Melissa, normally confident as can be, said she experienced "panic—sheer and utter panic." All of the negative thoughts entered into her mind—she was just a single location, why was he coming, would she be worth it, etc. That's when she made a decision. "I just showed up as me. Like, I'm not going to pretend that I am this MBA, perfectly schooled on all aspects of business. That's not what has made me successful. It's who I am as a leader and a human that's made me successful." This is exactly what refining your *roar* is all about—owning who you are in the face of potentially brutal and deeply challenging questions.

At the end of their meeting, he asked her if she had any questions for him. She asked what he was looking for in a partner. He replied, "Do you have a mirror?" That was the moment she realized that being confident in who she was had no downside.

The Aspen Group acquired the majority stake of Rejuv. Melissa took her proceeds, put enough away for the security of her family, and reinvested the rest with The Aspen Group to rebrand Rejuv to be Chapter Aesthetic Studio. They've opened twenty-two locations and counting.

Melissa joined the executive team at The Aspen Group to grow Chapter and is loving running a larger organization with the backing of a partner. She sees it as a long-term play.

"I am still so invested. I'm enjoying myself. I'm learning. I'm challenged every single day. But knowing that you have that choice, to continue to work, but you don't have to continue to work. You get to *choose* to continue. That is something I can't describe."

If Melissa had hesitated, or not taken the meeting because The Aspen Group was looking for multi-location medical spas, she might never have been able to experience that kind of freedom. It was only because she had the confidence to go for it, despite the fact that she wasn't a 100 percent perfect fit, that the deal got done.

Chapter Eleven

The Whisper Way

Casey and Renee filled the other women in on their plan, and they were met with cheers and applause. It was certainly a bold concept, and the collective group truly believed in that mother-daughter duo energy. Ramona asked them all to think about how *they* could be bold and push past their self-defeating thoughts in each of their own businesses. As Wendy participated, she thought about how much easier this was for her than it would have been prior to the retreat. She was learning. They all were.

"Ladies, I'd like you to all get your notebooks for our final exercise. You will need three pages, and you will need all of the clarity and confidence we have channeled throughout the weekend. Are you ready?"

They were.

"On the first page, I want you to write whatever comes to mind after writing: *Here is what I know for sure about this business.* I want you to answer not only from your head, but from your heart. Sit quietly and let the answer come to you; don't try to force it. As entrepreneurs, you couldn't have started your business without guts. And right now I want you to channel what's inside your gut. Start simple with things that you definitely know, like, *Our app is not functioning as well as it could be.*" Here she looked at Hannah. "Or you can go to something more based in feeling, like, *I want to build something incredible and long-lasting with my mom.*" She looked at Casey, smiling. "Just write what feels true."

The women started writing. Ramona didn't want to distract them with the next part of the exercise yet, as she saw they were in a space to take on this kind of challenge. And by the way, Ramona knew exactly how challenging this was. In order to connect with your own vision, she knew, you must be in a space to hear your own inner voice.

A long while passed, and the writing continued. Finally, all the pens were down.

"Now turn to the next page. And on the right side of the page, I want you to sketch a picture of yourself. It can be as rudimentary as you want. A stick figure, even. But I need an image that represents you."

For this one, Ramona got a couple of incredulous looks, but she watched as they reflected themselves on paper. She couldn't help but notice how stunning Phoebe's drawing was. That woman had such talent.

Pens down.

"Now that I've got you using the more creative side of your brain, on the other side of the page, draw seven circles. In the first circle, write a small letter *W.* The second, *H.* Continue until you've spelled *WHISPER.* Leave space in each circle to write after you've done that."

The women did as they were told.

"Next page, write *My FOCUS.* You're going to leave that page blank. When you leave here, I want you to think long and hard about what you've learned. I want you to look at what you know for sure. And I want you to fill in your circles on your plan. What is your why? How are you going to achieve it? What are the income targets? What makes you special? What is your profit target? How can you help build or grow your exec team? And finally, what do you need to do this all with unwavering confidence?

"The next page should contain immediate next steps for you to execute on that plan. That should become very clear once you fill in the circles. While the circles are forward facing and could be two, three, or ten years in the future, your focus should be based on what you need to do *right now* to get to your goals.

Ramona then passed out a piece of paper to each guest. On it were some sketches, and some areas for the ladies to fill in specific spaces.

"Once you've thought all of this through, you'll enter it into this plan. I call it the Whisper Way Vision Board." While your notebook pages are just for you, The Whisper Way is a strategic planning tool that is meant to be shared with your advisors, your team, or anyone who is helping you achieve these goals."

The plan is pretty, thought Wendy. It had all the elements of a typical strategic plan that she'd seen in her past business work, but it was infused with the feminine energy of Ramona, and it captured everything she knew she'd need to move forward.

"Another important part of this is having accountability partners. You will work with your executive team on the Whisper Way vision board. But for now, we are going to spend some time working on those three pages in your notebook, and I recommend you share them with each other when you're ready. This is our last exercise, so we will break for dinner once you all feel like you've started work on this. And, like I said, it's truly just a start. No matter where you are in your entrepreneurial journey, today is always a new beginning, and it should be treated with that kind of excitement, awe, and respect. I believe in all of you."

And with that, Ramona turned on the balls of her feet, and silently, slowly walked out of the room, tapping into her own *roar*. At dinner, she'd host the concluding event that would send these fantastic women on their way, and her first Whisper Retreat would be in the books.

The women all stayed to complete the assignment.

"Are we ready to rock?" said Sophia.

"We are ready to *roar*," said Elena.

They started writing, and sharing, and didn't stop until it was time to get ready for dinner.

······

The women arrived at dinner ready for the closing activity. It was funny—Ramona hadn't asked them to, but somehow each of the women wore their most elegant attire to the dinner. Perhaps they wanted to channel their newfound collective confidence, or maybe it was just because they knew it was the last time they'd be without kids, employees, and normal societal pressures for a while.

They had each come into this weekend unsure of what to expect. Now, they understood Ramona, her method, and, most important, how it could help them grow.

"I hope we are all feeling great now, and, most important, feeling clear," Ramona began. "You are an incredible group of women. I thank you for bringing your honest, true selves to this group. My hope is that you leave here with the beginnings of a plan that can help you turn these lifestyle businesses into life-changing assets, and based on what I've seen, I think you're there."

Just then, Casey did the unthinkable. She interrupted Ramona!

"Ramona," she said. "We'd like to propose a toast."

The server brought over nine glasses of (of course) red wine.

"Thank you for helping us figure out what the hell we want, and why we want it," Wendy said.

"Thank you for showing us that there is a path to get there, and that we can learn from those who have come before us," said Hannah.

"Thank you for sharing your incredible, inspiring story, and for protecting us by making sure our revenue is as strong as it could be." Ivy had a lump in her throat. She wished she could keep a little Ramona in her pocket at all times.

"Thank you for challenging us to think about what makes us different, and showing us that each of us has a unique story to tell." Sophia was thinking about how invaluable this was—and how she might have just quit and gone back to full-time homemaking if she hadn't made the time to come here.

"Thank you, thank you, thank you, Ramona. For showing us that money doesn't have to be the root of all evil, and that we can run beautiful, profitable businesses while still living out our damn purposes." Phoebe's head was swirling. She could write an entire novel about the artistry of Ramona.

"Thank you for getting us out of our own way. Thank you for breaking down our egos a bit—well, my ego, anyway. And thank you for showing us that a business of one might work for a while, but has a lot of risk that may not be worth the reward in the long run." Elena couldn't remember the last time she'd picked up her phone.

"And thank you, Ramona," said Renee. "Thank you for reconnecting me with my daughter in a deeper, more meaningful way. Thank you for connecting me with these women who have become like sisters. Thank you for teaching us to be unafraid to go big, and to use our collective voices to *roar!*"

The ladies held up their glasses. "To Ramona!"

"No," said Ramona, raising hers in turn. "To all of *you*."

Glasses clinked and the evening was officially in session.

On each plate lay a perfectly printed menu on a piece of stationery with "The Whisper Way" embossed at the top. Next to each setting was a pen and a place card, each of which had a saying printed on it:

Work On Your Why

Hone In on Your How

Improve Your Income

Secure Your Secret Sauce

Perfect Your Profit

Elevate Your Exec Team

Refine Your Roar

Whisper It into the World

Wendy looked at each of the pens, the stationery, and the entire aesthetic of the table, and thought to herself, *Ramona understands the power of detail.* She probably would have made a great stylist.

Ramona began the final exercise. "One time, I was at a conference, and a woman had me close my eyes and led me through a visualization exercise. She asked me to start by breathing, and then imagine that I knock on the door of my own house, five years from now. I answer the door, as me, from five years in the future. She asked many detailed questions. What did my house look like? What was I wearing? What did I say? For me this was pivotal, because I had a baby on my hip in my vision, and this was after several miscarriages. I decided to try again after that, and sure enough . . ." She opened the beautiful locket she was wearing and pointed to the picture of a child inside it ". . . there came Bella."

Sophia realized she had never asked Ramona a thing about her own children. Ramona was so focused on all of them, there was no time. But Sophia was glad to see that Bella was in her life. Ramona was probably a great mother.

"I also envisioned that I had sold my agency and left New York."

"Sure enough . . ." said Hannah, waving her arms around to show the farmhouse.

"Exactly. My point is, we know more than we think we do about what we want and why we want it. We just have to sit long enough in our own space, and remove distractions in order to find it.

"I'm not going to lead you through a full meditation. After the past couple of days, I don't think you even need it. You know how to eliminate distractions now, and to quickly get in a zone of quiet contemplation. That's really like a muscle. Snapping into that space will be much easier for you now, you just have to remember what it feels like."

Elena knew that was absolutely true. She hadn't looked at her phone once since the beginning of the trip. She hoped all of her clients weren't waiting to fire her when she got back, but even if they were, she'd rebuild, but the right way.

Ramona continued, "I want you to simply sit with yourself, and imagine you meet yourself just a few years from now. You are meeting up with 'future you' at a local coffee shop."

Renee yelled out, "Yes, we're all at Coffee MD in Omaha!"

"Who are you? What are you doing? How is your company doing? Have a real conversation with yourself, and pay attention to every little detail. Really envision it. And then? Pick up the pen in front of you and *write*. Write it all down. You've got ten minutes, ladies. Let's do this."

And just for effect, Ramona chimed a bell to get them in the zone.

They wrote. They wrote and they wrote and they wrote. A few of them were crying. When their pens were down, Ramona had them self-address an envelope of the same stationery and place the note in the envelope.

"This note will be mailed to you someday. And whether your life looks like what you wrote, or it turns out completely differently, I hope you remember that you took two days for yourself to realize what you wanted, and what your business needed."

Ramona clasped her hands together. For better or worse, this weekend was complete. She'd probably ask for surveys after it was done, but what was most important for her was that she was inspired. She'd build out The Whisper Group to be something incredible, even if it changed a lot along the way.

The dinner went long into the night with the women talking, laughing, and sharing. And in the morning, when they left, they each took a piece of the retreat with them. Ramona couldn't wait to see what each of them did, but she knew it would be a long while before she'd find out. Businesses aren't built over weekends. They're built over days and weeks and months and years of ups and downs and successes and failures and wins and losses. That was exactly what she loved about it.

Chapter Twelve

Three Years Later

"**E**veryone, come in here! I have to show you this!"

Elena instantly knew what the box was, the moment her assistant placed it on her desk. She couldn't wait to show the box to the other coaches at Wise Words. After all, it was the impetus for their hiring! Elena's business had grown enough that she could hire four coaches. She was making only marginally more money, but most important, she had people she could trust, and she could step away from work without feeling sick to her stomach.

"To my darling inaugural Whisper Way attendees . . ."

• • • • • •

Renee wasn't at the Omaha Coffee MD location when the box arrived, but Casey was. Renee was off at their Boise location, showing the newest manager how to set up shop. Renee was particularly excited about that location, since it was the third that they'd opened that had a mother-daughter team running it. The box was signature Ramona, filled with beautiful packaging, and pens, and some delicious goodies from the farm.

"A few years back, you gave me a tremendous gift."

. . . . . .

"I love that move, but try adjusting your hips a little to make your core more level."

Hannah had just onboarded the next influencer instructor. After building the app for two years on her own, she took on a partner, who was very connected in the influencer and events space. She'd recently added two influencers as instructors, forming the OurHour Collective, and her partner was helping plan out the first OurHour Tour—with Hannah at the helm as lead instructor. Hannah had just sold a health insurance company as a sponsor, as they were focused on helping underserved communities access tools to improve their mental and physical health. It had been a long road to get here, and she wasn't quite at the goal she had set, but as she opened the box, she felt like Ramona would be proud of her.

"The gift of sharing your stories, and workshopping your businesses with me . . ."

. . . . . .

Ivy thought back to when she received her first communication from Ramona three years ago. She had been at her wits' end. It was before she had built her signature "motion makers," a product that provided motion design on demand, before she had purposely reduced the contract of her monster client to take on more focused work, and before she had made the decision to complete the acquihire (a small acquisition where you simply take over the cost of the employee and their book of business) of her small competitor in order to take on competing business from the monster client's competitors.

It was also before she had considered selling to her employees as an option.

". . . and the gift of testing my Whisper Way method."

• • • • • •

Phoebe was paying her credit card bill when the box arrived. It felt good—she had paid her bill in full every month for a few years now and was carrying no debt. The business was growing slowly, but Phoebe's career as a speaker had really taken off, and a book deal was in the works.

The path wasn't exactly what she had plotted out with Ramona in their secret one-on-one convo, but she supposed that most plans are just that: road maps to follow. If you get a little lost along the way, you just take a detour.

"Because of you, I launched The Whisper Group, a strategic advisory firm for women founders, using a unique methodology that helps them from scale through sale."

• • • • • •

Sophia was returning from softball practice with Cole when she saw the box. The Whisper Retreat felt so long ago, it felt like she'd lived a thousand lifetimes since then. Sophia didn't regret the Whisper Retreat at all, even though she felt her result might be different than some of the other women. Sophia had sold WholeHeart at a slight loss shortly after she left Ramona's property. She'd looked at the numbers, and, most important, she looked at her own wants and desires. Sophia was obsessing about the business way more than she wanted to, and while she came out of the retreat with a road map for success, she realized that she wasn't going to be the one to take WholeHeart to the next level. She simply didn't want to. She researched some sites like Acquire.com and BizBuySell.com, and listed on a marketplace. She was able to sell to someone who wanted it more than she did. They decided to focus on direct-to-consumer selling versus retail sales and were experts in marketing. Sophia was happy that one of the buyers was a woman, and she felt resolved in her decision, mostly because of her own "why."

"*I wanted to share a little something with each of you. Check the envelope I've enclosed in the box.*"

. . . . . .

Wendy climbed off of her boat, and went into her house. She had moved out of Miami and had a much more laid-back life in the Keys. As she sifted through the box, she fingered the envelope in her hands and knew exactly what it was.

Wendy had recently taken a growth investment from a large department store chain, in a deal that valued Fashion Faire at $120 million. The plan was to integrate the app and its substantial user base and stylist data with the store's retail locations to differentiate their personal styling product. Wendy was all in on that growth, but she had stepped back from the CEO role and was now serving on the board, in addition to starting an incubator that helped provide capital and support to women and minority-owned startups. And Wendy had recently signed on as a guide for The Whisper Group, working with a group of women who owned online marketplace companies.

She was living the life she wanted, on the terms she wanted. And the best part was, she no longer had doubts about what she wanted.

"Love, Ramona"

Wendy opened the envelope, but she didn't need to. She knew exactly what was in it, and she remembered exactly what she had been thinking back then, and what she thought every single day until she finally achieved it.

It's five years later. I'm not in Omaha. (Sorry, Renee!) I'm in the Keys. I moved here after selling Fashion Faire last year. It took me four years to do it after that damn retreat with Ramona in her woods, but I did it. We sold to Saks after they sponsored our platform for their newly launched in-house stylist program. It was mostly a strategic acquisition: They didn't want other retailers to get to us, and they wanted to make their in-store experience more personalized (they had to, really, because retail is in the shitter). By the way, did I mention I look ah-mazing! I am relaxed and calm and I'm actually advising a startup incubator group. I know it's funny, since I refused to take venture money even after all those sharks tried to invest in me as I started to get traction. But this incubator really helps minority- and women-owned businesses, and I feel like I can help. Life is good, and I know who I am and what I want in a way that I wasn't able to see before.

• • • • • •

Ramona was barefoot, of course, as she walked through the grass on her property. She had just returned from shipping the boxes to her first "Whisper in the Woods" cohort. A lot had happened since then. The growth of The Whisper Group was unlike any experience she'd ever had, mostly because she followed her own Whisper Way to a tee. Ramona built a specific, repeatable methodology for scale. She herself had personally helped over two hundred women scale their companies in the past few years, twenty-six of whom used her as their M&A advisor when selling their businesses. She'd hosted annual retreats at the farm, which she did mostly for fun. But the real win was Ramona's plan to scale beyond her own skills. The Whisper Group was designed to keep things simple, and real, and provide women with bespoke solutions. But through her own journey, Ramona realized that her own time was not infinite for scaling. So she added another element to the promise of The Whisper Group. Ramona added eight guides like her—women who had sold their businesses and wanted to give back to other women like them. The secret sauce of that was Ramona's commitment to pairing women business owners with guides in similar verticals. For example, even though Ramona could work with a business of any kind, she now focused exclusively on services-based businesses. Wendy, whom she'd recently added as her ninth guide after she sold Fashion Faire, was working with marketplace businesses. The revenue split agreement allowed these women to make money while growing Ramona's core business. To date, The Whisper Group has helped over a thousand women, with over fifty-six M&A transactions because of that scale.

There were many moments in the journey where even the confident, composed Ramona had doubts. She would get in her head about the women's space being oversaturated. She would obsess about if she was just a glorified coach versus the inventor of a new method for women to scale their businesses. She would occasionally be in a situation where she felt out of her depth.

But she'd put one foot in front of the other, just as she had on the first day of that first Whisper Retreat, and kept moving forward. She used each and every part of the Whisper Way to drive her business forward.

And the best part? Not only did it work, but for the most part, Ramona was loving every minute of it. Even the hard parts. Even the mess. After all, that's business, and that's life. She was here for all of it.

Chapter Thirteen
Build Your Whisper Way Plan

At the beginning of this book, I spoke about the exit gap. That gap is real and it is true, and yet, we cannot and should not be defined by the fact that the cards are stacked against us. As you can see from the stories of the real (and imagined) women in this book, we can do incredible things.

In this section, I'm going to show you how to build your own Whisper Way plan. But first, I'm going to tell you that no one does this alone.

If we are going to do this, at the level that I know we can, we cannot do it alone.

To close the exit gap, we need support.

We need support from our families to evenly distribute household labor and childcare.

We need support from financial institutions and funders.

And we need support from one another.

Before we hop into how you can start to close the gap through your own business via the Whisper Way implementation guide, I thought I'd share some resources for help outside of your own business.

HOW CAN MY PARTNER/FAMILY CIRCLE HELP CLOSE THE EXIT GAP?

When you have more time to be intentional about growth, you will grow more. When you grow, you will increase your value at exit. According to the Global Entrepreneurship Monitor, which looked at women entrepreneurs across forty-nine economies, family responsibilities were listed as a common barrier to business operations.

How do we fix that?

Eve Rodsky is the author of the book *Fair Play: A Game-Changing Solution for When You Have Too Much to Do*. On her website, Eve writes that *Fair Play* "identifies the 100 main tasks in any partnership and then divides those tasks fairly (not necessarily equally!) so that both parties contribute their share." There's also a corresponding card deck that partners can use to divide and conquer. Often, it helps recognize that women generally shoulder more of the weight of domestic responsibilities and unpaid emotional labor.

Dave and I played the Fair Play card game. Afterward, I ended up giving away quite a bit of my unpaid labor to him and our kids (in age-appropriate ways). Now, Dave does the laundry, my daughters load and unload the dishwasher, and even my eight-year-old son sets the table and clears after dinner. These may seem like small things, but they add up to be huge. Relieving some of that responsibility freed up mental time for me in a way I had never realized that it could. That helped me to invest more brain power in my businesses—and recharge in a real way during off hours.

HOW CAN I FIND FUNDING FROM GROUPS COMMITTED TO HELPING CLOSE THE EXIT GAP?

There are definitely some institutions that are changing the game. For instance, there are some US Small Business Administration (SBA) loans that are specifically available for women-owned businesses.

IFundWomen is also an incredible resource. Founded by serial entrepreneur Karen Cahn, IFundWomen bills itself as "the go-to funding marketplace for women-owned businesses and the people who want to support them with access to capital, coaching, and connections." This platform allows women to crowdfund for their businesses, allowing for investments to add up substantially for founders.

If you'd like to try your hand at raising funds through venture capital, start with angel investing groups. Golden Seeds is an early-stage investment firm that focuses on funding and advising women-led businesses.

After the early stages of seed funding and angel investing can come Series A, B, and C funding rounds, which give outside investors the chance to fund you in exchange for equity or even partial ownership in the company. If you're ready to step into Series A or beyond, consider groups like the Fearless Fund. The fund is focused on investing in companies led specifically by women of color. Black women founders raise about 0.34 percent of all venture dollars. Funds like Fearless Fund are out to change that number, and they've already had some great wins by investing in companies like HairBrella and Ellis Island Tea.

HOW CAN WE COLLECTIVELY CLOSE THE EXIT GAP?

If, by chance, you are one of the women that has sold her business, congratulations. When I sold, I breathed a sigh of relief. I felt joy, I felt excitement, I even felt some sense of loss. I certainly felt accomplished.

But I also felt **compelled**.

I felt compelled to pay it forward.

None of us can do this on our own; it takes a village. And so, my ask of you, whether you've built a million-dollar business that you're running, or you've sold for $20 million-plus, is to spend a little time with the women who are following in your footsteps. Help guide them through, and remind them that they can do it, and that you're here as a sounding board.

I felt compelled.

And here is my attempt at giving back to you. A practical, tactical plan that incorporates personal vision, allowing you to exit for gobs of money if that's what you choose, or keep working in a business you love if that's what you choose.

Either way, the choice is yours.

Now let's get started.

IMPLEMENTATION GUIDE: HOW TO BUILD YOUR OWN WHISPER WAY

When I was growing my own company, I approached strategic planning with precision. I researched every available option for planning. I tried the one-page strategic plan from Verne Harnish's book *Mastering the Rockefeller Habits*. I tried the EOS system, and their strategic planning. I tried working with coaches. They all worked to some degree, but they didn't feel natural for me. I was someone who was easily distracted. Someone who was not formally trained in business, especially business finances. I was someone who was very focused on doing things "the right way," and so I went down a rabbit hole of trying to follow some of these systems verbatim. It just all felt very formal, and rigid, and, if I'm being honest about my experience, kind of male.

When I built the Whisper Way, it was designed for just me. But I came to realize there were a lot more founders like me than I thought. Founders who needed things to be simple, and speedy, and without a lot of pretense. Founders who wanted a snapshot of their plan, without diving too deep into the weeds. Founders who wanted to build a plan based on their own exit planning, in addition to their company's growth, and founders who wanted to build a company around the life they wanted, not a life around the company that they had.

The exercises accompanying the fable in this book are designed to help you get to your Whisper Way, which is a comprehensive, simple strategic plan for founders. Those exercises, versus a more traditional strategic plan (like EOS, for example), are designed just for you as the owner. You don't need to share every thought that you have about your own exit or income with your team. When those exercises and pre-work are done well, they become a feeder for a plan that you run with your exec team.

The Pre-Work

To begin your Whisper Way process, you are going to take some quiet time and prepare your notes and thoughts around each of the tenets of WHISPER. While I recommend that you use a Whisper Group advisor to take you through the steps, it was really important to me to democratize the process and make it accessible to all through this book. If you are not using an advisor, I recommend working with a mentor or one of the entrepreneurs you have seated at your "dining room table" from the How exercise (chapter 5). No matter what, it should be someone you feel comfortable discussing finances openly with.

For the purpose of teaching you how to build your own Whisper Way, I am going to use my own example of how I thought about The

Whisper Group, and I'm going to let you completely behind the curtain of my goals with this business.

WHY: For my *why*, I didn't need to bring as much prep work; I simply had to dig deep. I had already had an exit and was relatively secure. The answer I kept coming to was *legacy*. It was for my daughters, and for all women. I wanted to build a business that was exclusively for women (even if that pissed people off), that helped them make money, and that helped them close the gap in revenues and exit valuations for women-owned versus male-owned businesses. And to do that, I wanted to have an exit for The Whisper Group that felt "epic"—because it would make me money and signal to the market that women should be taken seriously. It would also, if done correctly, get millions more dollars into the hands of women, and it would *also* provide a big old suck-it to all the men along the way who told me that nothing was different for women-owned businesses. (Hey, sometimes parts of your *why* aren't always rational, but they're motivating!)

HOW: I needed to look at how much I wanted to extract from this business personally, but I also needed to look at the EBITDA it needed to generate and the typical multiples in the space. I did a deep competitive analysis, including competitors' pricing as well as exit data. I also came prepared with what I honestly wanted to make each year from the business. It was important to me to leave the money from my first exit as my dedicated retirement fund, and I wanted to draw enough out of the next business to cover my family's day-to-day expenses. I also worked with a close friend who was an advisor, who was unafraid to challenge me on all of this. I also had to be realistic and prepared that this whole earning money thing was going to take a while!

INCOME: Helping women-owned businesses who are learning to scale is not the most lucrative business, especially if I want to stay true to my commitment of helping them focus on profit. How could I price an offering that would allow me to have recurring revenue, but also scale, and have the kind of impact needed on the world? I built a diversified revenue stream of events, Whisper Way plans, and M&A advisory services, which is where I made the bulk of my income initially. In fact, I made a decision to charge lower amounts for Whisper Way planning, and then credit that entire amount back to the entrepreneur if I served as the advisor on her exit. I came prepared with my proposed pricing, and how many clients I thought I could service myself in a year, and I focused on how I could make her revenue recurring, expected, and diversified.

SECRET SAUCE: Prior to doing the exercise, I spoke to *everyone*. I spoke to clients and advisors and prospects. I spoke to women who were starting businesses and women who had exited businesses. I asked tons of questions, and I armed myself with the answers, prepared to solve prospective clients' greatest pain points. For The Whisper Group, I knew that women wanted to work with other women like them, who had done it before. With the proliferation of the "coaching" movement, women didn't know who to trust, so my guarantee of matching them with advisors in their vertical who had previously sold a business was necessary and key.

PROFIT: Since I had sold a business before, and I had the data from the "How" section, I knew what a healthy margin percentage should be. I also knew what I personally wanted to make. I had clear expectations about the expenses of the business, plus what they would expand to as I scaled my revenue, and I was armed with the target profit percentage. One interesting thing to note: Even though I had already exited and was secure, my profit margin targets were higher for The Whisper Group than they were for Likeable. That's because I had the learnings from the first business to know what I *could* do, and what I *should* do.

EXECUTIVE TEAM: I had a network that I'd spent decades developing, and there were many people who wanted to work with me and for me. But for this exercise, I focused primarily on myself. What were my weaknesses? Where did I need to be challenged? And, most important, as determined in the Secret Sauce section, what were the values I was hiring for? For me, this meant I needed people with more operational skill sets. I needed folks who would keep my ideas from going in too many different directions. I also kept in my mind that I wanted to make sure the business wasn't just all about me, which was a clear risk.

ROAR: I still had some work to do when it came to my *roar*. And that work really never ends, let me tell you. I wrote down every single doubt prior to the plan and asked myself, *How does this serve me?* Sometimes, doubts *do* serve us. For instance, I doubted that I could help a business in tech, because I lacked that experience. Even though I probably could have done it just fine, that led to the insight around hiring guides with specific expertise. But most of our doubts do not serve us. They end up holding us back from going for greatness. Either way, we can't tackle them unless we lay them out on the table and acknowledge them.

Perhaps you've already been doing the end-of-chapter exercises in this book, which is great! Maybe you haven't started yet, which is also just fine. If you have some exercises you've yet to complete, dedicate some time to exploring those. You don't necessarily have to do them in order, by the way, so if something is challenging you, set it aside and try another exercise first. This process is for *you*. Check them off as you complete them and keep your notes together.

- *Why* exercise, page 43
- *How* exercise, page 64
- *Income* exercise, page 83
- *Secret Sauce* exercise, page 101
- *Profit* exercise, page 117
- *Executive Team* exercise, page 134
- *Roar* exercise, page 150

After you do the pre-work, I recommend you step away for a day. Let it all settle.

When you come back, come with a pen and paper. Now it's time to write yourself a letter.

We call this letter "what I know for sure."

The Letter

For "what I know for sure," I want you to look at all the work you've done on the last seven exercises. Reread your insights in WHISPER order. It's important that *Roar* is last, because it's going to remove a lot of the doubt in your mind and get you to a space where you can do this. Here was my real "what I know for sure":

<u>What I know for sure</u>

When I sold my first business, I felt that there were experiences that were unique to me as a woman.

Through my many discussions with other women who scaled and sold their businesses, I found that they felt the same way.

I know that women have less access to capital, generally have a lower risk tolerance than men, and usually don't start businesses because of their financial acumen. I know that investment bankers, brokers, and advisors are paid handsomely on a financial transaction, but very few people if any deal with the emotional implications of that transaction.

I know that when people spoke to me about numbers in a macro way, I often felt confused, and I ultimately wanted to know what I would make at the end of the day—and I am not alone in that.

I know that I was afraid to say what I really wanted for most of my life. And I'm not afraid anymore. I know that I invented a methodology, and I have seen results for many.

I want this letter to be filled with what your gut is telling you. What you feel confident about when you are at your most calm and focused. What you envision for yourself and this business. And I want you to save that letter. Put it in a folder somewhere. And every time you feel doubt, simply return to what you know for sure.

The Whisper Way Vision Board

The Whisper Way Vision Board is a strategic plan that is designed to be shared with your entire team. You'll see that the seven tenets of WHISPER are here, except in this version of the plan, they are used to organize some of the more traditional components of a strategic plan that your team may be used to.

If your Whisper Way Vision Board were folded in half, the left side would remain rooted in WHY parts of your plan, meaning the ones that are more strategic. The right side would focus more on the HOW, meaning the ones that are more tactical in nature. On the Whisper Way Vision Board, your **WHY** specifically contains your core values, your big hairy audacious goal (BHAG), your brand promise, your income diversification, and your genius zone (often referred to as a sandbox). There are dozens of books that contain exercises for how to discover these, but my favorite is *Mastering the Rockefeller Habits* by Verne Harnish, even if it's not perfect.

Here are some simple tips for tackling each of the areas in the WHY section of your Vision Board.

Core Values: I've always used the Mission to Mars exercise when determining Core Values. In your team planning session, everyone pretends that you have to send five people from the company to Mars as ambassadors. The Martians don't speak English, so these five people will have to represent your group through their actions. When we did this for The Whisper Group, once everyone had their lists of the five people they would nominate, we shared them and talked about why we chose those particular employees. Our core values were the common attributes of these people.

BHAG: A big hairy audacious goal has to be monumental and future focused. So for this portion, I want you to picture yourself in the future. You've succeeded with this company beyond your wildest dreams. What does that success look like? When people talk about your company, what do they say? Are you featured in some incredible media publication? What does the headline say? Imagine it all. Try having the members of your team each write a small paragraph about your envisioned future and then read them out loud. Highlight what feels right, and look for commonalities as you listen around the room. Use those to help you solidify the BHAG.

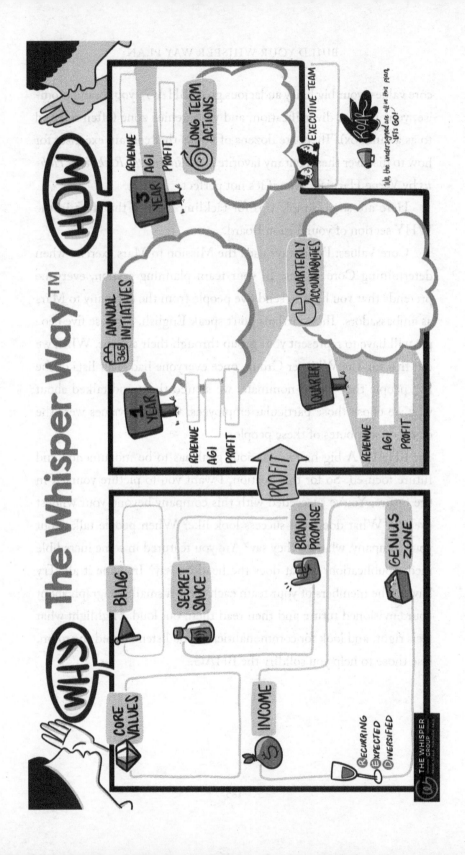

Your **INCOME** and your Genius Zone are designed to be completed together. Start with the genius zone, and think of it as your sweet spot: what you are really good at, and what people usually hire you for. Hopefully, it's already your primary product offering, but if not, maybe that's something to consider. Once you have your genius zone, head to the income section. This is where diversification comes in. Remember RED? How are you going to make sure you have products that are recurring, expected, and diversified? Explore some of those here as you build out your product road map.

Your **SECRET SAUCE** is all about the magic, and that's why we have your brand promise in this section. Your brand promise hangs out at the intersection of your purpose and your positioning.

Your brand promise connects back to your larger *why*. It's what your brand strives to achieve in the world. It's an idea that lives beyond any financial goals and doesn't speak to the methods, means, or specific approaches that you'll take to fulfill it.

Your brand promise also connects to why your customers value you. It has to reflect your positioning to customers. At Likeable, the social media agency I built, our brand promise was "faster service from the smartest in social, with Likeability guaranteed." And we lived it. It wasn't a slogan; it was a promise. Think about what you can guarantee your customers, and why that makes you special or different from your competitors. I recommend trying the Secret Sauce exercise in chapter 7 with your entire team.

Now head to the second half of the Vision Board, where it's time to get focused on how we are going to accomplish this. It is all about your timing, your steps, and financial metrics. For this to be rooted in reality, you'll want to come prepared with your expected revenue and expenses, as far out as you're reasonably able to forecast. This part of the plan examines what you'll execute in the next ninety days, the next year, and the next three years. And of course, in order to afford all of this, our **PROFIT** numbers are also located in this section.

For your **EXECUTIVE TEAM** and your **ROAR**, I want you to simply write the names of the accountable leaders at the org in the executive team box. For ROAR, I want every one of them to sign the plan, signifying buy-in and complete alignment.

And that, my friends, is your Whisper Way plan. If you do it right, you'll be making more money, feeling more in control, and building an asset that will fundamentally change your life.

This book was a labor of love. Part fiction, part workshop, part research, it is meant to guide you through this next chapter of your own journey. And now, it's time to head off into my own next chapter—the scaling of The Whisper Group. It's going to be a journey, one with highs and lows and everything in between. But whenever I feel alone, or afraid, or at a loss for what to do next, I will simply put on my caftan, crack open this book, and channel my inner Ramona. I hope you do, too.

For more information on developing deeper Whisper Way plans, and other free resources, visit:

WeAreTheWhisperGroup.com

Acknowledgments

I poured my heart and soul into this book, and I couldn't have done it without the help of so many women and their incredible stories. To the women who were featured on my podcast, and in this book, thank you. There are plenty of resources that glamorize the start of entrepreneurship for women, and many that talk about the perils of fundraising. However, I don't believe we've had a platform for women to tell their honest accounts of how their business stories end, and I feel so honored that you trusted me to tell your stories.

In addition to women who have exited, there are women who are building true behemoths that have not yet sold, but who have been loud champions in sharing these stories in the world. Thank you, Aliza Licht, Anat Baron, Cindy Gallop, Jessica Zweig, Amy Nelson, Shelley Zallis, Sallie Krawcheck, and Lexi Grant. There are many, many others.

We live in a different day and age, where books don't just "happen" for authors. It requires building a brand and a platform that is meaningful. I absolutely could not build that platform without my partner in content crime, Jose Betancourt, and the woman who makes me look good while filming, Perry Foulke.

ACKNOWLEDGMENTS

Writing this book was a real journey. It required sourcing and scouring for details with my apprentice, Lilly Conway. It required mini writing retreats with one of my nearest and dearest friends, Anita Rosner. It required daily reading reviews with my mentor Candie Harris, and my hero, Judy Fisher. It required Honey Cantrell to run Likeable for an entire month without me while I holed up in a corner and wrote. And it required the support of my agent, Jaidree Braddix, and of the entire BenBella team, specifically Claire, who learned how to speak Carrie, and Glenn, who took a huge chance on me, likely because Dave begged him to.

About Dave. There is no Carrie without Dave. You are my forever cheerleader, my champion, my partner, my inspiration, my hero. Thrilled to be forever #inittogether with you. Thank you.

And to Charlotte, Kate, and Seth. It's all for you guys.

Bibliography

INTRODUCTION

"Annual Women-Owned Business Study 2023." Biz2Credit, March 8, 2023. https://www.biz2credit.com/research-reports/annual-women -owned-business-study-2023

Elad, Barry. "Women Entrepreneurship Statistics." Enterprise Apps Today, June 28, 2023. https://www.enterpriseappstoday.com/stats /women-entrepreneurship-statistics.html

Exit Planning Institute. "2023 National State of Owner Readiness Report." *The Exit Planning Summit*, 2023. https://exit -planning-institute.org/hubfs/Member%20Center%20Resources /2023%20National%20State%20of%20Owner%20Readiness %20Report.pdf

Jucca, Lisa. "Female Entrepreneurs' Glass Ceiling is Intact." *Forbes*, March 8, 2023. https://www.reuters.com/breakingviews/female -entrepreneurs-glass-ceiling-is-intact-2023-03-08

Kapaun, Camille. "The Illusion of Venture Capital for Female Founders." *Forbes*, June 22, 2022. https://www.forbes.com/sites/columbia businessschool/2022/06/21/the-illusion-of-venture-capital-for -female-founders/?sh=23f618e374c6

Krawcheck, Sallie. "The State of Women's Financial Health." Ellevest, September 22, 2022. https://www.ellevest.com/magazine/news /financial-health-index-wellness-survey-annotated-press-release

Mathur, Priyamvada. "Charting Female Founders' Standout Year for VC Exits." Pitchbook, Feburary 17, 2022. https://pitchbook.com /news/articles/female-founders-venture-capital-exits-charts

Post, Corinne. "Private Equity Manages $10 Trillion with Few Women Decision Makers." *Forbes*, November 8, 2022. https:// www.forbes.com/sites/corinnepost/2022/11/08/pe-manages-10 -trillion-but-is-failing-its-diversity-equation-we-should-all-be -concerned/?sh=3fc1567053d2

Rubio, Jordan. "Female Founders Take the Good with the Bad in a Challenging 2022." PitchBook, December 18, 2022. https:// pitchbook.com/news/articles/2022-female-founders-year-in-review

Shah, Meera, and Poppy McMullan. "Trends in Female-Founded Exits over the Last Decade." Buzzacott, October 2, 2023. https:// www.buzzacott.co.uk/insights/what-are-the-trends-in-female -founded-exits-over-the-last-decade

"Small Business Loan Statistics: Is Sexism Prevalent?" Tayne Law Group, P.C., accessed April 12, 2024. https://attorney-newyork .com/business-loan-statistics/

Wells Fargo. "The 2024 Impact of Women-Owned Businesses." https://www.wippeducationinstitute.org/_files/ugd/5cba3e _96b999d23fb04d8eb488192a179781d4.pdf

CHAPTER 4

Gonsalves, Kelly. "What Is the Mental Load? The Invisible Labor Falling on Women's Shoulders." mbgRelationships, November 17, 2022. https://www.mindbodygreen.com/articles/what-is-the -mental-load

Kay, Katty, and Claire Shipman. *The Confidence Code*. Harper Business: New York, 2014.

Petrosyan, Ani. "Daily Time Spent Online by Users Worldwide Q1 2024 by Age and Gender." Statista, August 2024. https:// www.statista.com/statistics/1378510/daily-time-spent-online -worldwide-by-age-and-gender/

Saujani, Reshma. "Teach Girls Bravery, Not Perfection." TED, February 2016. https://www.ted.com/talks/reshma_saujani_teach _girls_bravery_not_perfection?subtitle=en

Team Asana. "Begin with the End in Mind to Maximize Your Potential." Asana, February 15, 2024. https://asana.com/resources /begin-with-the-end-in-mind

CHAPTER 5

Carlson, Nicholas. "Here's the Research Report That Inspired Sales force.com to Drop $700 Million on Buddy Media." *Business Insider*, June 4, 2012. https://www.businessinsider.com/heres-the -research-report-inspired-salesforcecom-to-drop-700-million-on -buddy-media-2012-6

"Valuation & EBITDA Multiples for Tech Companies: 2024 Report." FirstPageSage, May 23, 2024. https://firstpagesage.com/business /valuation-ebitda-multiples-for-tech-companies/

Zhou, Luisa. "Small Business Statistics: The Ultimate List in 2024." Zhou Ventures, Inc., May 9, 2024. https://luisazhou.com/blog /small-business-statistics/

CHAPTER 6

Cartin, Stephanie, and Courtney Spritzer. "Reaching for Excellence with Bea Dixon of The Honey Pot Company." *Entreprenista*, April 12, 2021. https://entreprenista.com/podcast/reaching-for -excellence-with-bea-dixon-of-the-honey-pot-company/

Kavilanz, Parija. "It Started in Her Kitchen. Now Her Products Sell at Target and Walmart." CNN Business, November 27, 2020. https://us.cnn.com/2020/11/27/business/the-honey-pot -company-fresh-money/index.html

Lee, Hannah. "Editorial: The Female Flame: The Significance of the Color Red to Women." *Los Angeles Times*, November 21, 2023. https://highschool.latimes.com/sunny-hills-high-school/editorial -the-female-flame-the-significance-of-the-color-red-to-women/

CHAPTER 7

Bilton, Nick. "Tinder Taps an Age-Old Truth." *New York Times*, October 30, 2014. https://www.nytimes.com/2014/10/30/fashion /tinder-the-fast-growing-dating-app-taps-an-age-old-truth.html ?_r=1

"Bumble Mission, Vision & Values." Comparably, accessed August 11, 2024. https://www.comparably.com/companies/bumble/mission

Kosoff, Maya. "Report: Ousted Tinder Cofounder Settled Her Sexual Harassment Lawsuit Against the Company for 'Just over

$1 Million.'" *Business Insider*, November 4, 2014. https://www
.businessinsider.com/whitney-wolfe-settles-sexual-harassment
-tinder-lawsuit-1-million-2014-11

Shontell, Alyson. "Ousted Tinder Cofounder Sues for Sexual Harassment, and She's Using These Nasty Texts as Evidence." *Business Insider*, July 1, 2014. https://www.businessinsider.com/tinder
-lawsuit-and-sexual-harassment-text-messages-2014-7

Tellis, Shannon. "Did You Know Bumble Was Originally Supposed to Be a Platform for Women to Exchange Compliments?" *Economic Times*, April 4, 2023. https://economictimes
.indiatimes.com/magazines/panache/did-you-know-bumble-was
-originally-supposed-to-be-a-platform-for-women-to-exchange
-compliments/articleshow/99172005.cms

Wolfe Herd, Whitney. "A Letter from Whitney Wolfe Herd, Bumble Founder and CEO." Bumble, accessed August 11, 2024. https://
bumble.com/en/the-buzz/a-letter-from-whitney-wolfe-herd
-founder-and-ceo

Wolfe Herd, Whitney. "How I Built a Tech Company with Women in Control." *Forbes India* (blog), March 8, 2023. https://www
.forbesindia.com/blog/technology/whitney-wolfe-herd-how
-i-built-a-tech-company-with-women-in-control/

CHAPTER 8

Habiger, Sandra. "Profit and Loss Statement: Definition, Types, and Examples." FreshBooks, July 22, 2024. https://www.freshbooks
.com/hub/reports/profit-and-loss-report

Hasan, Zoya. "Wondering About Next Steps After Falling Out with Your Partner? Here's What Worked for This Founder." *Inc.*,

April 12, 2023. https://www.inc.com/zoya-hasan/fall-out-with -business-partner-next-steps-buy-them-out.html

"How It's a 10 Haircare Founder Carolyn Aronson Built a Multimillion Dollar Empire | The One | Forbes." YouTube video. Posted by "Forbes," April 4, 2021. https://www.youtube.com/watch?v =SE5gE9gUH4A

McGrath, Maggie. "The One Who Changed Everything for It's a 10 Haircare Founder Carolyn Aronson." *Forbes*, April 5, 2021. https://www.forbes.com/sites/maggiemcgrath/2021/04/05 /the-one-who-changed-everything-for-its-a-10-haircare-founder -carolyn-aronson/?sh=6f7fc0606450

"QuickBooks Survey: More Than 40 Percent of Small Business Owners Identify as Financially Illiterate." Business Wire, November 13, 2014. https://www.businesswire.com/news/home/2014 1113005240/en/QuickBooks-Survey-More-Than-40-Percent -of-Small-Business-Owners-Identify-as-Financially-Illiterate

Runnels, Carlyn. "Carolyn Aronson." Ideamensch, June 21, 2018. https://ideamensch.com/carolyn-aronson/

CHAPTER 9

Dhinga, Naina, Andrew Samo, Bill Schaninger, and Matt Schrimper. "Help Your Employees Find Purpose—or Watch Them Leave." McKinsey, April 5, 2021. https://www.mckinsey.com/capabilities /people-and-organizational-performance/our-insights/help-your -employees-find-purpose-or-watch-them-leave

Gupta, Sangeeta. "Why Hiring for Cultural Fit Can Derail Your DEI Efforts—and What to Do Instead." *Forbes*, September 17,

2021. https://www.forbes.com/sites/forbescoachescouncil/2021
/09/17/why-hiring-for-cultural-fit-can-derail-your-dei-efforts
---and-what-to-do-instead/?sh=1a88c2b9728a

Lagorio-Chafkin, Christine. "How a Former Ad Exec Built a $110
Million Business by Catering to How People Really Want to
Work." *Inc.*, October 10, 2022. https://www.inc.com/christine
-lagorio-chafkin/we-are-rosie-stephanie-nadi-olson.html

Olson, Stephanie Nadi. "5 Leadership Lessons from My First 5
Years as a Founder and CEO." We Are Rosie, February 21, 2023.
https://wearerosie.com/the-write-up/pov/5-leadership-lessons
-from-my-first-5-years-as-a-founder-and-ceo/

"We Are Rosie Partners with Align Capital Partners to Accelerate
the Flexible, Inclusive Future of Work." Newswire, December 21,
2021. https://www.newswire.com/news/we-are-rosie-partners
-with-align-capital-partners-to-accelerate-the-21582397

CHAPTER 10

Digitale, Erin. "Positive Attitude Toward Math Predicts Math
Achievement in Kids." Stanford Medicine News Center, January
24, 2018. https://med.stanford.edu/news/all-news/2018/01/positive
-attitude-toward-math-predicts-math-achievement-in-kids.html

Hardy, James, Aled V. Thomas, and Anthony W. Blanchfield. "To
Me, to You: How You Say Things Matters for Endurance Performance." *Journal of Sports Sciences* 37, no. 18 (2019): 2122–2130.
https://doi.org/10.1080/02640414.2019.1622240

Park, Sang-Hyuk, Bong-Suk Lim, and Seung-Taek Lim. "The Effects
of Self-Talk on Shooting Athletes' Motivation." *Journal of Sports*

Science & Medicine 19, no. 3 (2020): 517–521. https://www.ncbi
.nlm.nih.gov/pmc/articles/PMC7429435/

Richards, Louisa. "What Is Positive Self-Talk?" *Medical News Today*,
March 18, 2022. https://www.medicalnewstoday.com/articles
/positive-self-talk?fbclid=IwAR3PD-pnnARl

Shadinger, David, John Katsion, Sue Myllykangas, and Denise Case.
"The Impact of a Positive, Self-Talk Statement on Public Speaking Anxiety." *College Teaching* 68, no. 1 (2019): 5–11. https://doi
.org/10.1080/87567555.2019.1680522

CHAPTER 13

"About *Fair Play*." EveRodsky.com, accessed August 11, 2024. https://
www.everodsky.com/fair-play

"About Us." IFundWomen, accessed August 11, 2024. https://www
.ifundwomen.com/about-us

"GEM 2022/23 Women's Entrepreneurship Report: Challenging Bias
and Stereotypes." Global Entrepreneurship Monitor, November
14, 2023. https://www.gemconsortium.org/report/gem-20222023
-womens-entrepreneurship-challenging-bias-and-stereotypes-2

Wishart, Jessica. "BHAG Exercise: How to Have the Right Discussions to Get to Your BHAG." *Rhythm Systems*, August 6, 2020.
https://www.rhythmsystems.com/blog/how-to-have-the-right
-discussions-to-get-to-your-bhag

About the Author

Carrie Kerpen is the founder and CEO of The Whisper Group, the #1 Exit Readiness Advisory Firm for Women-Owned Businesses. Prior to launching The Whisper Group, Carrie started (and scaled) Likeable Media, a women-led digital agency, which Crain's named the 6th Best Place to Work in New York City. After successfully navigating the sale of Likeable to 1,200-person technology firm 10Pearls in 2021, Carrie researched The Exit Gap, producing an annual report on the disparities in exit values of female-led companies. She is the author of *Work It: Secrets for Success from the Boldest Women in Business*, as well as the host of *The Exit Whisperer*, a podcast featuring women who have sold their businesses. Carrie is also a Certified Exit Planning Advisor (CEPA) and lives in Port Washington, New York, with her husband, her three children, and her dog Homer.